ST ANTONY'S PAPERS · NUMBER 18

★

SOUTH ASIAN AFFAIRS

NUMBER TWO

ST ANTONY'S PAPERS
published by Messrs Chatto and Windus Ltd

★

NO.   I SOVIET AFFAIRS: ONE   (out of print)

NO.   2 FAR EASTERN AFFAIRS: ONE   (out of print)

NO.   3 THE ITALIAN LOCAL ELECTIONS 1956

NO.   4 MIDDLE EASTERN AFFAIRS: ONE

NO.   5 THE DECLINE OF THE THIRD REPUBLIC

NO.   6 SOVIET AFFAIRS: TWO

NO.   7 FAR EASTERN AFFAIRS: TWO

NO.   8 SOUTH ASIAN AFFAIRS: ONE

NO.   9 INTERNATIONAL COMMUNISM

NO. 10 AFRICAN AFFAIRS: ONE

NO. 11 MIDDLE EASTERN AFFAIRS: TWO

NO. 12 SOVIET AFFAIRS: THREE

NO. 13 THE RIGHT IN FRANCE 1890–1919

NO. 14 FAR EASTERN AFFAIRS: THREE

NO. 15 AFRICAN AFFAIRS: TWO

NO. 16 MIDDLE EASTERN AFFAIRS: THREE

published by Oxford University Press

NO. 17 MIDDLE EASTERN AFFAIRS: FOUR

ST ANTONY'S PAPERS · NUMBER 18

SOUTH ASIAN AFFAIRS

Number Two

THE MOVEMENT FOR NATIONAL FREEDOM IN INDIA

EDITED BY

S. N. MUKHERJEE

OXFORD UNIVERSITY PRESS

1966

Oxford University Press, Amen House, London, E.C.4

GLASGOW NEW YORK TORONTO MELBOURNE WELLINGTON
BOMBAY CALCUTTA MADRAS KARACHI LAHORE DACCA
CAPE TOWN SALISBURY NAIROBI IBADAN
KUALA LUMPUR HONG KONG

PRINTED IN GREAT BRITAIN
BY BILLING AND SONS LTD., GUILDFORD AND LONDON

CONTENTS

1 Introduction   9
   by S. N. MUKHERJEE

2 Moderates and Extremists: two attitudes   19
   towards British rule in India
   by D. ARGOV

3 The Idea of Freedom in the political thoughts   34
   of Vivekananda and Aurobindo
   by DENNIS DALTON

4 Nationalist Interpretations of *Arthaśāstra* in   46
   Indian Historical Writing
   by JOHANNES H. VOIGT

5 Lord Curzon and Indian Nationalism,   67
   1898-1905
   by S. GOPAL

6 The Effects of the Russian Revolution on   74
   India, 1917-1920
   by ZAFAR IMAM

7 Nehru and Early Indian Socialism   98
   by DEITMAR ROTHERMUND

30168

The main emphasis of the work of St Antony's College, Oxford, since its foundation in 1950 has been in the fields of modern history and international affairs. The College organizes a number of regular Seminars at which are read papers produced by its members in the course of their research or by visiting experts from other institutions. The College further sponsors the delivery of lectures in Oxford by scholars of international reputation in their respective fields.

An appreciable volume of contribution to scholarship is thus being produced under the auspices of St Antony's and the present series was started in order to preserve and present a selection of this work. The series is not, however, confined to this material alone and includes contributions from other places.

Two numbers a year are issued and each number is devoted to a particular topic or a particular part of the world.

INTRODUCTION

By S. N. Mukherjee

IT IS VERY difficult to say how the future historian will describe the age in which we now live, but it is certain that he will be struck by the sudden end of European domination of the world after the Second World War. Between 1945 and 1960 no less than forty countries with a population of 800 millions revolted against the colonial powers and gained freedom, while another 600 million Chinese (under the Communist leadership) emerged as a great power in world politics. Since 1960 many more African countries have won independence. Such dramatic and revolutionary changes have never taken place before in human history.[1] It is almost certain that to the student of the history of the second half of the twentieth century no single theme will be more important than the rise of Afro-Asian nationalism. It is not so much because the majority of mankind live in these areas as that the fall of Europe from a position of dominance marked the beginning of the decline of the old economic and social system, namely capitalism. This meant a complete social and economic change and a shift of emphasis in power politics from north-west Europe and America to the new emerging nations. This does not imply that the process of change is now complete and that capitalism has ceased to exist. But what is significant is that the classical capitalist system, its political philosophy, liberalism, and all the social and moral values it stood for are undergoing a profound change. However, it does not necessarily follow that socialism as known in the Soviet Union is replacing world capitalism everywhere. In fact ever since the death of Stalin the Soviet system itself has been going through a process of readjustment. The validity of orthodox Marxism–Leninism is being challenged even in the Soviet Union. It is not possible to prophesy the future shape of the world, but it is clear that the rise of Afro-Asian nationalism marks the beginning of a new era in human history.

It is generally conceded that the emergence of India is one of the

[1] For a new analysis of this historical change see G. Barraclough, *An Introduction to Contemporary History* (London, 1964), pp. 148–94

major factors in the development of Afro-Asian nationalism. India was one of the first nations to gain freedom, the Indian movement for national freedom was one of the oldest and most experienced, and it was used as a model by many other nations of Africa and Asia. The work of Gandhi and the Indian National Congress attracted world-wide attention, but it was especially in Asia and Africa that many young men were inspired by Gandhi's work and adopted his methods and organization in their struggle for freedom. Many African nationalist organizations even adopted the name "Congress".[2]

So it is natural that there should be widespread interest in India and her recent history. The political development of modern India is so complex, and the material so abundant, both in Britain and in India, that the numerous works that have appeared in recent years have not yet exhausted the possibility of many more new interpretations of this dynamic change. Every year since about 1950 there have appeared new monographs and new articles dealing with various aspects of Indian nationalism; various theories are now being put forward to explain the origin and nature of this phenomenon; and various models are being suggested to research students and scholars to help them probe further into the question of the rise of modern India. That the growth of nationalism in India is an indirect result of British rule and the impact of Western education is beyond dispute. But what is yet to be answered is how British rule brought about this profound social and political change in India. What agencies played the vital role? How far did the traditional norms condition the Western impact on India? Did the British officers working as guardians consciously use their time and energy to mould the destiny of India, or was the British raj an unconscious tool of history? It could be argued that the civil service was the Western agency primarily responsible for the social change. It could also be argued that the introduction of a market economy, with private property in land and freedom for the unrestricted exploitation of India by British commercial interests, was the greatest single factor in the development of modern India. Here I do not propose to give a definite answer to any of these questions, nor do I intend to examine all the answers provided by other scholars. I shall only endeavour to examine very briefly some of the accepted views on Indian nationalism and tentatively suggest a possible strategy for research on the subject.

The terms "nation" and "nationalism" have so much emotive force in them that they defeat any attempt to make a scientific definition.

[2] T. Hodgkin, *Nationalism in Colonial Africa* (London, 1956), p. 146

However, it is clear that nationalism is a name given to a movement of a group of people attempting to gain political freedom from the domination of another group of people for a territory which they consider to be their homeland. It is a relatively new phenomenon in human history. It came to Europe at the beginning of the nineteenth century and to India about eighty years later. But the political agitation is the culmination of social and economic change: in Europe it was no doubt the direct result of the "double revolution" (the Industrial and the French). In India it was the culmination of the process of social change that had been taking place ever since the emergence of the British power in Bengal in the middle of the eighteenth century. It is easy to dismiss Indian nationalism, as some of the British officers did, unless one is ready to probe deeply into the social and economic causes of the rise of the new classes in India. For India is too vast and diverse to conform to the European models of nation and nationalism. To the British officers, the Congress and its middle-class leaders who professed liberalism and asked for the introduction of self-governing institutions in India, appeared to be a microscopic minority created by the English universities in India and cut off from the rest of the population. John Beames, an Indian civilian, one of the last to attend Hailey-bury, perhaps echoed the sentiments of his class when, in 1883, he wrote about the controversy over the Ilbert Bill:

> "There has been growing up, of late, a class of natives who though numerically few have become, by their extravagant pretensions and excessive self-conceit, by unreasonable and unsatisfied longing for power, and by their morbid discontent and disloyalty, a serious danger to the stability of our rule in India . . . It is a pity that so much weight is attached to the opinion of these people. They are doubtless very clever and write and speak very eloquently. But all their opinions are in truth nothing but place-hunting and power-hunting, more or less artfully disguised."[3]

So nationalism in India was dismissed as an agitation of a group of "place-hunters" who had no following among the masses. In 1901 Lord Curzon was comfortably hoping to assist Congress to a "peaceful demise".

The British historians of this period either ignored the growing national movement or regarded it only as an ephemeral phenomenon.

[3] Barun Dé, "Brajendranath De and John Beames: a study in the relations of patriotism and paternalism in the I.C.S. at the time of the Ilbert Bill", *Bengal Past and Present*, lxxi (Jan.–June 1962), pp. 15–18

Smith in his *Oxford History of India* (1911) failed to mention the Congress and their demands. Sir H. Verney Lovett in volume vi of the *Cambridge History of India* grouped the political agitation of the extremists with crimes. To British historians the development of radicalism in Bengal was merely the result of the failure on the part of the district administrators to tackle a handful of disgruntled Bengali Hindus. Verney Lovett wrote:

"Altogether there was a mass of discontent, social, political, and economic, which gave ample opportunity for revolutionary teaching. The conspirators had gained a long start and spread their nets widely. Murders and boycotting of witnesses and informers had broken down some prosecutions and were building up terrorism. The great water country of Eastern Bengal was stirred during those critical years 1906–1909. The views of numbers of imaginative young Hindus regarding the British were moulded, not by any personal contacts with individuals, but by scurrilous newspapers, distortions of history, and the idea that while a millennium was struggling on the threshold its entry was blocked by a foreign government."[4]

While Sir H. Verney Lovett assailed the extremists, his colleagues, writing in the late 1920s in the same volume of the *Cambridge History of India*, found the old explanation of Indian nationalism as a minority movement quite inadequate. Some held up the moderates as the most sensible political group in Indian politics and looked upon the gradual constitutional development in favour of the Indians as inevitable.[5] Professor Dodwell, the general editor, suggested that modern Indian history should be looked upon as the great British effort to "transform into an organic state the inorganic despotism which the Crown had inherited from the Company and the Company from the former Indian governments".[6] According to Professor Dodwell modern Indian political development owes nothing to her traditional society; it was wholly created by the British and the new middle classes who were the product of English education and British rule.

"Therefore when the rising class of Indians began to demand political reform and when the British government began to consider how best to give effect to this demand neither side could turn for

[4] *C.H.I.* vi. 559. It is interesting to compare the charges of intimidation and terrorism made by the white minority government in Rhodesia against the African Nationalists (1965)

[5] *C.H.I.* vi. 538–47   [6] *C.H.I.* vi, vii

guidance to Oriental political experience and were compelled to make their plans on the alien idioms of the West."[7]

Sir John A. R. Marriott writing in 1932 put this theory rather bluntly:

"It is undoubtedly true that a wave of 'nationalism' has been sweeping over Asia, and has reached India, but that wave would have lapped the shores of India calmly, almost imperceptibly, had not the people or some of them, already passed through many stages of preparation. Such nationalism as exists among the peoples of India is merely the product of the policy persistently pursued by British administrators. English is in India the *lingua franca* of revolution. Dalhousie began the work of material unification."[8]

This thesis that Indian nationalism was the product of the administrative policy pursued by the British officers was thoroughly worked out by later historians. They were less arrogant than Marriott and less anxious about the future of India without Britain.[9] L. S. S. O'Malley thought that Britain's mission was to give India "the best form of government that it was capable of giving and India was capable of receiving".[10] Throughout the nineteenth century India enjoyed the rule of benevolent despots, whose sole purpose was to provide an efficient and just government. However, after Curzon the administration was held as a trusteeship, where Indians were trained in the techniques of self-rule. According to L. S. S. O'Malley, although the principle of Indian participation in matters of Indian politics was recognized in the constitution of the Legislative Councils in 1861 it was only in 1917 that the British government announced a desire to develop a government in India based on democratic principles.[11] Sir Reginald Coupland held similar views.[12]

Since the last world war Professor C. H. Philips of the Department of History, School of Oriental and African Studies, University of

[7] *C.H.I. vi, vii*

[8] Sir John A. R. Marriott, *The English in India: A Problem of Politics* (Oxford, 1932), pp. 307-8

[9] Marriott wrote: "We are asked to place the government in other hands which we believe will be less just, less strong and less efficient. It is no light thing to require an imperial race to surrender the pride of achievement and to sacrifice the fruits of it; to fling the India that it has nursed up to adolescence into the witches' cauldron, knowing not what will emerge therefrom." Op. cit., p. 308

[10] L. S. S. O'Malley (ed.), *Modern India and the West* (London, 1941), p. 587

[11] O'Malley, op. cit., pp. 598-9

[12] Sir Reginald Coupland, *India: A Re-sattement* (London, 1945), pp. 71-90

London, and the research scholars working under his guidance have
generally upheld the thesis of Dodwell, Marriott, O'Malley, and
Coupland. Nationalism in India is regarded as entirely a product of
British policy and English education. From Professor Philips's point of
view the Independence Act of 1947 is merely the culmination of the
evolutionary process which started with the emergence of British
power in India. The history of modern India has so far been presented
to us as the history of British India. It is merely a summary of the State
Papers, such as the despatches between the Home Government and the
Government in India, and the private papers of British families with
Indian connections; they deal with such problems as administrative
policy, factional feuds among officers, and the workings of the various
pressure groups in the House of Commons with interests in India.
The Indians, particularly in the eighteenth and the nineteenth centuries,
have a very small role in the Indian history of Professor Philips and
his colleagues. In a recent work Professor Philips has set out to
answer certain questions concerning the history of modern India.
To him the fundamental question is: "How was Britain's civilizing
mission to be accomplished, in what ways were Indian minds to be
opened, and how were the poor ignorant millions to be raised from
the dust?"[13] This approach does not allow the Indians any initiative in
changing the future of their society, and all that is good in India today
is considered to be the result of the "British civilizing mission". To
say the least, this approach ignores the complex problems of the adapta-
tion of traditional institutions and ideas to the new development.
Our attention is directed to British policies and to the problems of
implementing such policies. At times we are also told of the Indian
reaction to them but we know very little about the reforms introduced
by the Indians themselves and about the struggle that Indians waged
against social and religious conservatism.

Thus, in the textbooks of Indian history, Lord Bentinck is given
credit for stamping out superstitious customs like suttee and thagi, as
a champion of enlightenment and liberalism. The atmosphere created
by the agitation and movement led by Raja Rammohan Roy against
such superstitious customs is generally ignored. The British suppressed
suttee at least ten years after Rammohan started his movement in 1818.
In fact Professor Philips and his colleagues have denied heroism to the
leaders of modern India. They tend to belittle the Indians, their struggle
for religious and social reforms in the nineteenth century, and their
political struggle and their sacrifices in the twentieth century. If

[13] C. H. Philips, *The Evolution of India* (London, 1963), p. viii

nationalism were purely the product of the British administration, the best thing for the Indians to do would be to co-operate. The logical implication of this thesis is that the mass movement, the emergence of Gandhi, Nehru, and Bose, was unnecessary, if not a real hindrance to the progress of "the self-governing institutions in the country".

Professor Philips may score a point or two against some of the nationalist historians who have a tendency to be uncritical about their leaders, but this can hardly satisfy an enquiring mind. It is not my intention to deny the impact of the West and the British administration on modern India. But the history of India cannot be understood solely in terms of the Western impact, as this fails to explain the immense dynamism of Indian society; we cannot in these terms understand how India withstood the cultural challenge of the West and showed an amazing vitality which proved wrong all the old theories about its being a stagnant society. Nor can we learn why all the Indian leaders from Rammohan to Gandhi insisted that all their plans for social reforms were not innovations but were to be found in early India, so that they had to dig out passages from classical Indian texts to gain sanction for their actions. In other words, if we think that nationalism was solely the product of British rule, not only do we belittle the achievements of the Indian leaders but we take away a full dimension of Indian history, by underestimating the role of the traditional society and institutions in moulding modern India. We shall then be asked to reject Indian political ideas as secondhand and shall fail to distinguish between borrowing and assimilating. Vivekananda did not just borrow the Christian idea of service, but he grafted it on to the Indian idea of asceticism. Similarly, old institutions such as the caste system survived, constantly readjusting themselves with the changing times. India also inherited a complex administrative system from the Mughals, especially in relation to the collection of land revenue. The British kept many features of the old system, and it has a lasting influence on the modern Indian organization of land and taxation.

So nationalism in India was not a minority movement, though it did not strictly conform to the European models, nor can one understand its origin and nature solely in terms of British administrative policy and English education. Clearly we need to evolve another methodology to understand this phenomenal development in human history.

I have already said that the political struggle for freedom was a culmination of the social change in India which started in Bengal during the second half of the eighteenth century. In other words nationalism in India is a product of the disruption of the old economic and social order. This disruption took place, not because the British set out to change the destiny of India, but because of the growth of a market society, the process of which was accelerated by the establishment of British rule. A market society may be described as a society in which the production and distribution of goods and services is regulated by the market. In such a society each individual's capacity to labour is his own property and is alienable. Land and resources are also owned by individuals and are also alienable.[14] Such a society through the free market in land and labour provides opportunities for individuals to acquire unlimited wealth and power and thus alter their social position. This is an ideal-type, but the basic features of such a society could be found in Europe since the days of Mercantile Capitalism.

It is not possible in this introduction to depict, even in outline, the growth of the market society in India. It is sufficient to say that it was somewhat related to the establishment of the British Raj in Bengal during the second half of the eighteenth century. During the course of the nineteenth century the market society and the British power spread throughout the subcontinent. British trade penetrated the country, and the new land regulations changed the entire way of life. Such regulations did not create a new set of rights; for the ownership of land as a *de facto* right was already in existence in many parts of India, and it was recognized by many English officers before Cornwallis.[15] But the regulations clearly defined such rights, and what is more important is that such regulations made land an alienable and a saleable commodity for a large market, and so allowed capital to purchase an unlimited amount. Thus through the land settlements and through extensive trade the British helped the growth of a market economy in India.

The direct effect of the growth of this market society was a large scale social mobility which had never taken place in India before. It changed the very basis of the interrelationships between individuals and between social groups. This created a new social élite, who became more wealthy and increased in number from the middle of the eighteenth century onwards, who lived in Calcutta and other administrative and trade centres, and could not be fitted into the traditional social stratification. Those who could earn enough wealth or achieve some intellectual standing through the new English education could be

[14] For a definition of a market society see C. B. Macpherson, *The Political Theory of Possessive Individualism: Hobbes to Locke* (Oxford 1963), pp. 53–61
[15] S. N. Mukherjee, "Sir William Jones and the British attitudes towards India", *J.R.A.S.* parts i and ii, 1964, pp. 37–47

accepted as members of this élite. Although members were mainly Hindus, caste did not play an essential part in selection. They raised their economic status through trade and commerce, as subordinate agents of the Company and private British traders, or as middlemen or moneylenders. They were a group who recognized their new status, which they owed to the new economy and the British rule, and, in Bengal, they called themselves *bhadralok* (gentlemen). This was not a purely economic group, as there were very rich and not so rich *bhadraloks*; nor was it another caste, but a new social class.

The political development of modern India since the beginning of the nineteenth century can be considered as the history of the struggle of this class to find a new identity. As the traditional norms which kept the old society together seemed inadequate to the new élite, a new code of behaviour was required. This is one reason why there was such a wave of social and religious reforms in the nineteenth century and later a demand for political reform by the new middle classes.

There is now a tendency among a number of Indian historians to explain the history of modern India in terms of the political idioms of this élite. Many works on the "freedom movement" are now being written solely based on the political writings of the leading Indians and the British officers. But this method ignores the social mobility which created the élite; some of the Indian historians fail to see that the market economy created a social erosion, which affected the very basis of the old society. In other words there was a constant shift of status at all levels. Although the masses came to the political arena only after the emergence of Gandhi in 1920, the movements for social and religious reform had been going on throughout the nineteenth century, even among the lower orders. The aims of such movements were different from the aims of the middle-class movements, and they expressed their demands through traditional channels. This social mobility may be considered the positive response to the growth of the market society, while the peasant revolts, heroic as they were, were a negative response to this development.

So, to study the political development of modern India since the nineteenth century, one has to use not only the methods used by European historians in their study of the modern sophisticated political movements in Europe, such as the Movement for Parliamentary Reform in Britain or the Nationalist Movements on the Continent, but also the methods which are normally used for the study of pre-industrial societies and primitive rebels. In other words, we should not use one single model but a combination of many models, for otherwise

B

there is a danger of putting too much emphasis on one aspect and ignoring the others. Thus we might be led to say that the movement at the village level, expressed through traditional channels, was more important than the movement in the towns, expressed through modern channels (the Press, meetings, etc.). In fact both were important, and they were interconnected, each influencing the other.[16] There is also the other danger of ignoring the role of ideas in history and explaining the national movement solely in terms of power politics and competition for offices among various pressure groups and classes.

Clearly the problem is far more complex than is generally realized. It is not possible for one man to cover the whole period within a short time. The present volume is a selection of papers which were submitted to a seminar held at St Antony's College during the Trinity Term, 1964. Each author has chosen his own subject which he thought important and used the methods which he considered most useful. It should not be considered as a definitive study of the subject but as a sample of various interpretations of the movement for national freedom in India now being given by different scholars working in different universities throughout the world.

I am most grateful to the Fellows of St Antony's College in helping to organize the seminar and the publication of the papers. I am also grateful to the contributors for their co-operation, and my wife's help has been invaluable in the preparation of the volume.

[16] Professor Morris-Jones has recently described contemporary Indian politics as a tale of three political idioms, modern, traditional, and saintly. This was perhaps true for Indian politics in the nineteenth and early twentieth centuries. See W. H. Morris-Jones, "India's political idioms", in C. H. Philips (ed.), *Politics and Society in India* (London, 1963), pp. 133–54

MODERATES AND EXTREMISTS:
TWO ATTITUDES TOWARDS
BRITISH RULE IN INDIA

D. Argov

THE INDIAN NATIONAL CONGRESS was formed in 1885 under the guidance of a group of liberal-minded Englishmen, which included A. O. Hume and Sir William Wedderburn. At the beginning it was a small body consisting mainly of lawyers, journalists, and teachers, with modest aims. It was concerned with presenting an image of respectability and loyalty to the Indian Government. An exclusive body of English-educated Indians whose principal desire was to assimilate Western political institutions, the Congress kept aloof from the masses.

The Congress directed its main effort towards England and pinned its hopes on the Liberal party. It justified its requests for Indian representation in the British Government of India on the basis of England's pledges to India. The concept of England's pledges was built upon declarations of Thomas Munro, Macaulay, Henry Lawrence, and above all upon Queen Victoria's proclamation, as enhanced by Ripon's pro-Indian policy. But, from the end of Ripon's viceroyalty in 1884 to the August Declaration in 1917, successive viceroys and secretaries of state for India emphatically repudiated the feasibility of introducing English political institutions to India. The statement by John Seeley: "A time may conceivably come . . . to leave India to herself, but for the present it is necessary to govern her as if we were to govern her for ever",[1] proved to be the consummation of England's pledges and their delayed fulfilment.

The Congressmen appealed to Englishmen in England and placed their reliance on English history and English political ideas; they claimed social equality on the grounds that they were British subjects. The present tendency in some Indian historians to depict the early history of the Indian National Congress as the history of the Freedom Movement ignores the fact that the moderate leaders of the Congress

[1] Sir John Seeley, *The Expansion of England* (London, 1883), pp. 193–94

19

constantly harped on the theme of securing the permanence of British rule in India. For Banerjea, *Swaraj* meant self-restraint;[2] Sinha and Gokhale said that, if the British were to leave India, Indians would call them back before they reached Aden.[3] They reconciled loyalty to England with Indian patriotism, believing that the two were necessarily compatible and complementary.

During the end of the last decade of the nineteenth century, an uneasy feeling among a group of Congressmen could be noticed. This group began to doubt the efficacy of constitutional agitation and the so-called British mission in India. While the early Congressmen used English political ideas as their weapons for arguments and petitions, the new group bolstered up India's past and advocated militant struggle, not debate. This group came to be known as the Extremists, and Bal Gangadhar Tilak, Lajpat Rai, Aurobindo Ghosh and Bipin Chandra Pal were the chief exponents of the new group. However, men like Dadabhai Naoroji, Pherozshah Mehta, Gopal Krishna Gokhale, and Surendranath Banerjea remained loyal to the methods of constitutional agitation and aspired to attain Indian self-government within the British Empire. These men came to be known as the Moderates.

The growth of the Extremist party in India was explained by Bipin Chandra Pal: "Lord Ripon was a kind Viceroy but one who acted as a baby-comforter, and we had been brought up for too long a period upon political lollipops; Lord Curzon threw the baby-comforter away and thus made us feel our hunger for Swaraj."[4] At the same time it was the failure of the Moderates to gain reforms by persuasion which resulted in the Extremists' determination to force the government to yield power by coercion.

Both the Moderates and the Extremists came from the middle class, both were reacting towards British rule, and both voiced Indian grievances. The Extremists demanded social equality and political emancipation as their birthright. They drew sustenance from India's heritage and appealed to Indians by invoking religious partiotism; they disparaged the constitutional agitation of the Moderates as "mendicancy" and their stress on apprenticeship as an acceptance of ceaseless political servitude. Instead they called for self-reliance and self-apprenticeship through *swadeshi*, boycott and passive resistance.

[2] S. N. Banerjea, *A Nation in Making* (Oxford, 1925), p. 125

[3] Sinha to Lady Minto, Mary, Countess of Minto, *India, Minto to Morley* (London, 1934), p. 298. Cf. Gokhale to Lord Hardinge, Lord Hardinge, *My Indian Years* (London, 1948), p. 115

[4] B. C. Pal, *Speeches at Madras* (Madras, 1907), p. 6

For the Extremists Indian patriotism and loyalty to British rule were two diametrically conflicting entities. While the Moderates tenaciously sought gradual reform and could see no halfway-house between order and revolution, the Extremists held that revolution was but rapid evolution, and that peace and order under British rule amounted to national stagnation. Thus the differences between the Moderates and the Extremists were not confined to methods of agitation; their ultimate aims were fundamentally different. This paper seeks to outline the change in India's reaction to British rule from the period when the British Government of India was regarded as a providential government, ordained to fulfil a mission, to the time when it was viewed as a "Satanic government".

The Moderates believed that, prior to the establishment of British supremacy in India, their country suffered from a perpetual state of political anarchy. Although they paid lip-service to their Indian heritage, they were avowed admirers of Western political values. They held the concepts of equality before the law, of freedom of speech and Press, and the principle of representative government, as incomparably superior to their traditional Hindu polity which they generally termed "Asiatic despotism".

But while the Moderates believed that British rule was destined to accomplish its providential mission, they argued that the British Raj was "more Raj and less British" in the sense that it fulfilled the fundamental functions of Hindu kingship in preserving external and internal peace, but was reluctant to introduce English parliamentary institutions. The implicit faith of Congressmen in the efficacy of England's mission and their expectation of benefiting from its results were expressed by Madan Mohan Malaviya:

> "Representative institutions are as much a part of a true Briton as his language and his literature. Will . . . Great Britain deny us, her free-born subjects, the first of these when by the gift of the two latter she has qualified us to appreciate and incited us to desire it?"[5]

In the presidential address of the Thirteenth Congress, Shankara Nair re-emphasized the characteristic features which made Congressmen loyal, and frankly explained:

> "From our earliest school days, the great English writers have been our classics; Englishmen have been our professors in colleges; English history is taught us in our schools; the books we generally

[5] Report of the Second I.N.C. (Calcutta, 1886), p. 107

read are English books which describe in detail all the forms of English life; week after week English newspapers, journals and magazines pour into India. We in fact now live the life of the English."[6]

Under these circumstances, Shankara Nair asserted, Congressmen were animated by English political ideas and it was but natural that they sought political representation, but they fully realized that the fulfilment of their political aspirations were inseparably linked with the continuance of British rule. These declarations reiterated the conviction of loyal Congressmen that there could be no halfway-house between order and anarchy. The British Government of India maintained law and order, and any suggestion, open or veiled, of overthrowing it immediately raised to Congressmen the spectre of anarchy. However, the loyal proclamations went only as far as to reassure the Government that the Congress presented no danger to British rule, and at the termination of his Viceroyalty Lord Elgin declared: "The Empire of India has been won by the sword and must be held by the sword if need be."[7]

The partition of Bengal was announced on 20 July 1905 and took effect on 16 October 1905. A new province called Eastern Bengal and Assam was created by the merging of Assam with the divisions of Dacca, Chittagong, Rajshahi (without Darjeeling), and the District of Malda.

The partition was regarded by Bengalis not as an isolated measure but as the climax to Lord Curzon's unpopular policies. Hence it was taken up as a cause on which were fastened all the social, economic, and political grievances which had accumulated by 1905. It evoked an unprecedented wave of protests which unleashed the *Swadeshi* and Boycott movement and led to the formation of the New party in the Congress.

Swadeshi and Boycott were the outstanding features which distinguished the anti-partition agitation from any former Indian protest against the policy of the Government of India.

While Lord Curzon lampooned the anti-partition agitation in March 1905 as "petty volcanoes who scream and screech and throw their torrents of mud into the air",[8] in October the Viceroy wrote:

[6] Report of the Thirteenth I.N.C. (Amraoti, 1897), p. 9

[7] *Speeches by the Earl of Elgin* (Calcutta, 1899), p. 419. Farewell Speech at United Service Club, Simla, on 14 October 1898

[8] Curzon to Brodrick, EUR. MSS. F.111/164, 23 March 1905

"The agitation is now being conducted by methods of open terrorism and violence. It has been converted . . . into a purely political movement organized by a small disloyal faction."[9]

Gokhale presided over the 1905 Congress. The most important declaration in his presidential address was:

"The goal of the Congress is that India should be governed in the interests of the Indians themselves, and that in the course of time a form of Government should be attained in this country similar to what exists in the self-governing Colonies of the British Empire."[10]

Referring to the anti-partition agitation, Gokhale praised *Swadeshi* but cautioned against Boycott. He explained that the term "boycott" meant "a vindicative desire to injure another" and emphasized that "such a desire on our part as a normal feature of relations with England is of course out of the question".[11] While Gokhale advised restraint, Madan Mohan Malaviya emphatically declared that the Congress did not advocate the Boycott in Bengal and that it opposed the spread of Boycott to other provinces.[12] In contrast, Lajpat Rai impressed upon Congressmen that Boycott ushered in "the dawn of a new political era for India". He further stated:

"I must tell you that the message which the people of England wanted to send you through me was the message that in our agitation and in our fight and struggle for liberty we ought to be more manly than we have been hitherto. Englishmen hate beggary, hence it is our duty to show Englishmen that we are no longer beggars, and that we are subjects of an Empire where people are struggling to achieve that position which is their right by right or natural law. The Bengal spirit of protest has to be commended to other provinces of India. If the other provinces will follow their example, the day is not far distant when England will grant our rights. If you simply go there [to England] as a beggar without the consciousness of your power to demand your rights, you go there simply to be rejected. As friends of order we warn the Government, let it remember, and let you gentlemen also remember, that people once awakened cannot be put down. It is impossible for British rule after a century of liberal education to put us down like dogs and slaves. Why be

[9] Curzon to Brodrick, EUR. MSS. F.111/175, No. 452, 9 October 1905
[10] Report of the Twenty-First I.N.C. (Benares, 1905) p. 13
[11] Ibid. p. 11
[12] Ibid. p. 72

loyal? Once the policy of Boycott be adopted prepare for the consequence. Do not behave like cowards."[13]

Throughout 1906 the anti-partition agitation gathered momentum in Bengal and its repercussions widened the gulf between Congressmen. The chief exponents of Boycott were Brahma Bandhab Upadhyay,[14] Bipin Chandra Pal and Aurobindo Ghosh. Their sources of inspiration were the writings of Bankim Chandra Chatterjee (1838–94) and the preaching of Narendranath Datta (1863–1902) – better known as Swami Vivekananda. An example of Vivekananda's condemnation of slavish imitation of Western standards is reflected in the following extract from his essay on modern India written in 1899.

"When I see Indians dressed in European apparel and costumes, the thought comes to my mind perhaps they feel ashamed to own their nationality and kinship with the ignorant, poor, downtrodden people of India . . . Oh India! with this mere echoing of others, with this base imitation of others, with this dependence on others, this slavish weakness . . . will you attain by means of your disgraceful cowardice the freedom deserved only by the brave and heroic? . . . You the brave one, be bold, take courage, be proud that you are an Indian and proudly proclaim 'I am an Indian, every Indian is my brother' . . . Say brother 'the soil of India is my highest heaven, the good of India is my good' and repeat and pray day and night, 'O thou Lord of Gauri, thou Mother of the universe, vouchsafe manliness unto me.' "[15]

The historical novels of Bankim Chandra Chatterjee provided an additional major source of inspiration, notably his *Anandamath* and its poem *Bande Mataram*. "The Mother" was represented, chiefly by Aurobindo Ghosh, as a concept which expressed at once both the divine motherland and the mother-goddess in the form of Durga.[16] "The Mother" and the slogan "Bande Mataram" thus conveyed both patriotic and religious devotion. They generated mass emotional appeal which the academic Congress and its rational principle of constitutional agitation could not, and did not intend to, arouse.

[13] Report of the Twenty-First I.N.C., pp. 73–4

[14] Editor of *Sandhya*

[15] *The Complete Works of Swami Vivekananda*, Almora, iv., 412–13. Cited in *Sources of Indian Tradition*, ed. De Bary, pp. 658–9

[16] "The Durga Puja and Patriotism" – "The Motherland is no other than divinity itself . . . the Motherland in all her beauty and splendour represents the goddess Durga of our worship." *Bande Mataram*, 9 October 1907

An open split was forecast in the Congress when the hitherto un-consolidated groups of conservative and radical Congressmen con-verged into two opposite factions. The veteran leaders and their followers became styled the "Old party" or "the Moderates", while "the New party" led by Tilak, Lajpat Rai, Bipin Chandra Pal and Aurobindo Ghosh became known as "the Nationalists" or "the Extremists".

In 1907 between January and May, Tilak, Lajpat Rai, Bipin Chandra Pal and Aurobindo Ghosh set out to canvass support for the new party. The common denominator in their speeches and writings was an emphatic assertion that the belief in England's providential mission proved fallacious. They disparaged the Moderates' plea for Indians' equality of rights as British subjects, and emphasized that Indians were subjugated people whose rights for equality and liberty rested solely on the basis of fundamental human rights as enunciated by the French Revolution.[17]

Tilak presented the relationship between Indians and the Govern-ment of India in terms of power politics between rulers and ruled. He emphasized that politics were void of benevolence, and that history never recorded an instance in which an Empire ceased to exercise its rule by conceding its dominion voluntarily. In Tilak's words,

"At present we are clerks and willing instruments of our oppres-sion in the hands of an alien Government. The new party wants you to realize the fact that your future rests entirely in your own hands. If you mean to be free, you can be free; if you do not mean to be free, you will fall and be forever fallen. So many of you need not like arms, but if you have not the power of active resistance, have you not the power of self-denial and self-abstinence in such a way as not to assist this foreign government to rule over you? This is boycott, we shall not have their goods, we shall not give them assist-ance to collect revenue and to keep the peace. We shall not assist them in fighting beyond the frontiers or outside India with Indian blood and money. We shall not assist them in carrying on the administration of justice. We shall have our own courts and when time comes we shall not pay taxes. Can you do that by your united efforts? If you can, you are free from tomorrow."[18]

[17] The *Bande Mataram* published "La Marseillaise" with translations in English, Sanskrit, Hindi, Urdu, Bengali, Marathi and Gujarati, on 29 July 1907
[18] "The Tenets of the New Party", speech at Calcutta, 2 January 1907. I.O.L. tract 1010

Lajpat Rai upheld *Swadeshi* and Boycott as the religion of new India, the manifestation of self-sacrificing patriotism, the means of moulding a self-reliant Indian nation, and the spearhead of India's national struggle against British rule.[19] Discarding the Moderates' "sermons of unswerving loyalty", he asserted that it was folly to interpret India's status of political subservience as a beneficial school for political apprenticeship.[20] To emphasize this assertion, Lajpat Rai offered two scholarships for Punjabi students to study "methods of political work" and stipulated that they should undertake not to seek their career in the Government of India.[21] Outstandingly among Indian leaders, Lajpat Rai stressed the need to arouse the political consciousness of the urban workers and pointed out that "the wage-earning classes in this country gradually realize that their destiny and bread is in their own hands and not in the hands of those handful of people who overlord them".[22]

Implicit in the Extremists' rejection of petitions and appeals to the British Government was an underlying rejection of Western values and ideals. Bipin Chandra Pal contrasted the old and the new spirit of Indian patriotism in the following words:

"We loved the abstraction we called India, but we hated the thing that it actually was. Our patriotism was not composed of our love for our own history, literature, arts and industries, culture and institutions, but as a prototype of England which we wished her to be. The new spirit cured us of an imaginary and abstract patriotism. Love of India means a love for its rivers and mountains, for its paddy fields and its arid sandy lands, its towns and villages and poor people, for its languages, literature, philosophies, religion, culture and civilization."[23]

Pal denied the efficacy of constitutional agitation by arguing that the Government of India was not a constitutional government, in the sense that it rested on its own laws which did not bind it to recognize any constitutional rights of the people it governed.[24] Like Lajpat Rai, he

[19] "The Swadeshi Movement", *Indian Review* (May 1906), pp. 353–6
[20] " The National Outlook", *Modern Review* (March 1907), p. 205
[21] *Punjabee*, 6 and 20 March 1907
[22] Home Prog. Political 7590, July 1907
[23] "The New Patriotism", speech at Madras, April 1907, B. C. Pal, *Swadeshi and Swaraj* (Selection from Pal's writings and speeches during 1902–1907) (Calcutta, 1956), p. 9
[24] Ibid., p. 133

rejected the Moderates' emphasis on the indispensability of political apprenticeship under British guidance, and argued that British rule constituted India's bondage and as such could never be a school for freedom.[25]

Having thus rejected the Moderates' method of constitutional agitation and in particular its emphasis on apprenticeship under British guidance, Bipin Chandra Pal and Aurobindo Ghosh advocated boycott in the form of "passive resistance". Pal defined passive resistance as "non-aggressive active resistance" or "even the determination to allow a man beat you is the activity of one's will power";[26] while Aurobindo Ghosh defined it as "lawful abstention from any kind of co-operation with the Government".[27]

Outlining the practical form of passive resistance, Aurobindo Ghosh urged boycott of British goods and the sole use of *Swadeshi*; boycott of Government-controlled schools and the establishment of independent schools teaching "national education"; boycott of courts of law and the administration of justice through popular arbitration; and lastly, boycott of Government offices, police and army and the establishment of "national league of defence".[28] The double-edged purpose of passive resistance thus aimed to paralyse the executive functions of the Government and to foster a self-sustained popular system of administration.

Although Tilak, Lajpat Rai, Bipin Chandra Pal and Aurobindo Ghosh were unanimous in disparaging the methods of the Moderates, they differed in projecting the ultimate aim of Indian self-government.

Tilak explained self-government as the possession of Indian control over the administrative machinery,[29] but he by no means advocated the severance of India from the British Empire. "Our remote ideal", he declared, "is a confederacy of the Indian provinces possessing colonial self-government with all imperial questions set apart for the central government in England.[30] His dispute with the Moderates was limited to the application of different methods of agitation, but he conceived the same goal as that of the Moderates – a self-governing India within

[25] "The New Patriotism", speech at Madras, April 1907, p. 55
[26] "The New Movement", speech at Madras, April 1907; B. C. Pal, *Swadeshi and Swaraj*, p. 79
[27] Aurobindo Ghosh, *The Doctrine of Passive Resistance* (first published in *Bande Mataram*, 9–23 April 1907) (Pondicherry, 1948), p. 40
[28] Ibid., p. 70
[29] "The Tenets of the New Party", speech at Calcutta, 2 January 1907. I.O.L. Tract 1010
[30] Henry Nevinson, *The New Spirit in India* (London, 1908), p. 72

the Empire.[31] While the Moderates looked forward to a limited target of Colonial self-government, Tilak projected the ideal of *Swaraj*, yet he was at pains to explain its exact political meaning and confessed "at this stage it could not be determined what form of self-government we wished, it will be decided in thirteen or fourteen years hence".[32] He could better define *Swaraj* by emphasizing that it neither meant the expulsion of Englishmen, nor the breaking away from the Empire.[33] Above all he advocated continued loyalty to the Crown.[34] For all the image of Tilak as "the father of Indian unrest", his imprisonment in 1908 did not check the spread of terrorism, while on his release in 1914 he strongly condemned acts of terrorism, praised the "inestimable benefits which British rule conferred upon India by its civilized methods of administration", and called upon Indians to support England in the war.[35]

On the other hand, Lajpat Rai, Bipin Chandra Pal and Aurobindo Ghosh rejected the methods of the Moderates as well as their aim of Colonial self-government. For them, conciliation between Indian patriotism and loyalty to the Empire was anathema, and the ideal of self-governing India within the Empire a contradiction between two incompatible entities. "How can a subject race governed by another be patriotic towards its rulers?" asked Lajpat Rai.[36] He condemned Indians who celebrated "Empire Day" as "hypocrites who dragged Indian patriotism into the mire",[37] and bitterly denounced Indians who hankered after British honorary titles as "white sepulchres full of rotting corruption; the symptoms and disease of the national organism; the morbid parasitic cells which develop mean selfishness and thrive on favouritism".[38] While the Moderates polarized stability and anarchy, Lajpat Rai justified unrest as an essential harbinger of progress, and emphasized that India's release from political slavery necessitated her going through a "hell of unrest".[39] In 1914 Lajpat Rai praised acts of terrorism as "expressions of genuine passion for national liberty"[40]

[31] Henry Nevison, *The New Spirit of India*, p. 73
[32] "Our present situation", speech at Allahabad, 4 January 1907. I.O.L. Tract 1010
[33] Ibid., p. 73   [34] Ibid.
[35] *Indian Review* (Sept. 1914), p. 719
[36] "Indian patriotism towards the Empire", *Indian Review* (Jan. 1907), p. 52
[37] Ibid.
[38] "Title hunters", *Punjabee*, 27 January 1907
[39] "Political work in the Punjab", *Punjabee*, 13 October 1906, Home Prog. 7590, July 1907
[40] Lajpat Rai, *Autobiography*, p. 4

and unlike any other Indian leader, asserted that Indians should not support England in the war as mercenaries.[41]

Bipin Chandra Pal denied the feasibility of a self-governing India within the Empire on the grounds that India constituted the pillar of the Empire and therefore could exert effective self-government only if the Empire itself ceased to exist.[42] In addition Pal emphasized the racial division and expressed his conviction that Indians could never exercise self-government within a larger political framework which included Englishmen, Australians and Canadians.[43] On the basis of these contentions Pal advocated *Swaraj* in terms of "autonomous Government, absolutely free from British control".[44] He visualized the ideal of a self-governing India as a federation comprising republican states and constitutional monarchies in a democratic United States of India.[45] In projecting this ideal, Pal approvingly envisaged a transition period of inner conflict which entailed imposition of dictatorship and the temporary abandonment of democracy.[46]

Aurobindo Ghosh gave the clearest exposition of *Swaraj* by declaring it synonymous with independence – "a free national Government unhampered even in the least degree by foreign control".[47] To him, arguments about the liberalization of Legislative Councils or the wider admission of Indians to the civil service were futile and irrelevant. He upheld the view that the more reactionary the Government of India was, the more it stimulated Indians to abandon their acquiescence, and the more it spurred them to revolt. He justified revolution against British rule partly on the grounds that "liberty is the life birth of a nation and when the life is attacked by violent pressure, any and every means of self-preservation became right";[48] but more importantly, on the grounds that it was essential for Indians to go through a revolution in order to purge themselves from Western tutelage. To launch the revolution Aurobindo Ghosh advocated the creation of a "central force" to represent "the national will". In his words,

"There can be no genuine progress carrying the whole nation forward unless there is a central force representing either the best thought and energy of the country or else the majority of its citizens

[41] *Tribune*, 14 November 1929. "Congress Politics in 1914"
[42] "The New Movement", speech at Madras, April 1907. B. C. Pal, *Swadeshi and Swaraj*, p. 29
[43] Ibid., p. 152   [44] Ibid., p. 153   [45] Ibid., p. 203
[46] Ibid., p. 204
[47] Aurobindo Ghosh, *The Doctrine of Passive Resistance*, p. 17
[48] Ibid., p. 17

and able to enforce the views and decisions of the nation on all its constituent members."[49]

Or in short: "National reforms and national progress needs the organization of the national will in a strong central authority."[50] Unlike Bipin Chandra Pal, he avoided the term dictatorship, yet his idea of the "central force" representing the "national will" harbours the elements of dictatorship. Moreover, he conceived the ultimate aim of India's national emancipation as "a sacrifice to the Motherland, offered in feeding her fire, even with the blood, lives and happiness of our nearest and dearest".[51]

The anti-partition agitation in Bengal and the unrest in the Punjab during 1906–07 contained revolutionary elements which were far more militant than the relatively crude agitation during the Ilbert Bill controversy in 1883; yet in spite of the fact that by 1907 the nascent nationalist movement was fanned by religious fervour and spurred by racial animosity, as well as by economic distress and by political frustration, there was no Indian revolution.

Apart from the obvious reason that the military strength of the Government posed a formidable deterrent, while in contrast the Extremists had neither the resources nor the organization which could sustain a revolution, the main cause may be attributed to the political apathy of the peasantry, but more precisely to the fact that authoritative leadership centred in the Congress, and the Congress was dominated by Moderates who abhorred the prospect of a revolution. The Congress formed and represented a class of professional men whose political career, economic prosperity, and social prestige were either dependent on, or directly linked with, the existing institutions of the Government; their struggle was designed to increase their association with the Government, not to jeopardize their vested interests in a struggle against the Government. Hence the application of militant agitation instead of constitutional agitation had to be first fought out in the Congress itself, before it could have been effectively directed against the Government. In other words, the Extremists had first to capture the Congress in order to invest their militant ideas with an aura of authority which would attract a wider following.

Aurobindo Ghosh justified the impending clash on the grounds that a political struggle of subjugated people demanded an inner

[49] The Doctrine of Passive Resistance, p. 2
[50] Ibid., p. 4   [51] Ibid., p. 77

struggle rather than an appearance of fictitious unity. He relied on the examples of the Italian and American revolutions and concluded that in the struggle between the Moderates and the Extremists, "one or the other must be crushed or prevail before true unity of a regenerated nation can replace the false unity of acquiescence in servitude".[52]

The cleavages between the Moderates and the Extremists led to the 1907 Surat split which resulted in the expulsion of the Extremists from the Congress.

As an aftermath to the affray in Surat, P. Chandra Roy, editor of the *Indian World*, wrote: "We must realize the ideal of discipline *before* we can hope to realize the greater ideal of *Swaraj*".[53] But in 1911 he observed that because of its rigid constitution, the Congress had become an exclusive organization which "degenerated into a mere platform for glib oratory and claptrap declamation".[54]

Yet the Congress adhered to its creed, which was re-emphasized by Bhupendranath Basu thus: "We desire self-government not by revolution but by gradual evolution and we are prepared to advance steadily and surely, though it may only be slowly."[55] Gokhale expressed the hope in October 1908 that in ten years' time Indians would attain provincial self-government and explained: "It is no use trying to overthrow the present administration before we have something to put in its place."[56]

On the other hand, Aurobindo Ghosh protested:

"Nations that became free did not first convince themselves to be helots and then seek freedom. They denied they were servile, they laid down they were free, would become free, and became free."[57]

He contended that English political ideas of democracy were centred on materialism, and that English temper and culture were the very antipodes of Indian temper and culture. Hence he concluded: "If India is to model herself on the Anglo-Saxon type she must first kill everything in her which is her own."[58] He blamed the Moderates for the Surat split and asserted that the Extremists fought at Surat

---

[52] *Bande Mataram*, 27 October 1907
[53] *Indian World* (Jan. 1908), "The Lesson of Surat", p. 103
[54] Ibid. (July 1911), p. 109
[55] Ibid. (Jan. 1908), "The Indian Political Outlook", p. 5
[56] W. C. Blunt, *My Diaries* (London, 1919), ii, p. 229
[57] "On the Present Situation", speech at Poona on 19 January 1908. I.O.L. Tract 1044
[58] Aurobindo Ghosh, *Ideals Face to Face*, May 1908. I.O.L. Tract 1044

against the oligarchic and arbitrary rule of the Moderate leaders, whose insistence on their self-veneration, their obstinacy, reactionary conservatism and parochial policy, stifled the national movement. He further blamed the Moderates for having framed the rigid constitution which prevented the admission of popular leaders to the Congress and rendered it an undemocratic body.

The enthusiastic expression of the 1914 Congress of support for England in the war was dimmed by the end of 1916. The war and its many-sided effects produced a complete transformation in the attitude of Indians towards British rule and towards the hitherto acknowledged superiority of the West.[59] The change coincided with the death in 1915 of the three most prominent leaders of the Moderates: Pherozeshah Mehta, Gokhale and Subramanya Iyer. The 1915 Congress was still dominated by the Moderates; yet without Pherozeshah Mehta and Gokhale, it could no longer keep out the Extremists who entered the Congress in 1915 and swelled its ranks.

At the 1916 Lucknow Congress, the Extremists headed by Tilak, Gandhi, Annie Besant and Bipin Chandra Pal wrested the control of the Congress from the Moderates. "The Congress", Tilak declared, "had done its work as a deliberate body."[60] He called for action and voiced the demand of the Congress for Home Rule, i.e. India to be a self-governing Dominion in which Indians would have control over the Central Legislative Council with the exception of military matters and foreign affairs, and complete Indian control over all matters in the provincial government.

Until 1915 the Moderates' Congress voiced national aspirations, but it was an exclusive body whose watchword was caution. From 1916, the Congress was still composed of lawyers, journalists, teachers and merchants, yet, under the control of the Extremists, it became the national forum and constituted the vanguard of militant nationalism.

The 1917 Calcutta Congress met under the glow of the August declaration. It was presided over by Annie Besant whose election to the presidency was a successful challenge to Banerjea's leadership in Bengal.[61] The session clearly marked the undisputed control of the Extremists over the Congress under the leadership of Lokamanya Tilak, Mahatma Gandhi and C. R. Das.

While the details of the proposed Montagu–Chelmsford reforms

[59] See Percival Spear, *India* (University of Michigan Press, 1961), Ch. xxxi, pp. 337–46
[60] Report of the Thirty-first I.N.C. (Lucknow, 1916), p. 85
[61] Hamndranath Das Gupta, *Deshbandhu Chittaranjan Das* (Delhi, 1960), p. 35

were worked out in London, in India the recommendation of the Rowlatt Report to try seditious cases without juries or witnesses was enacted in January 1919. Mahatma Gandhi's declaration of hartal, his arrest, the riots in the Punjab, the Amritsar massacre, and above all the vote of approval of repression by the House of Lords, resulted in Gandhi's insistence upon disassociation from the "Satanic" Government of India.

C

THE IDEA OF FREEDOM
IN THE POLITICAL THOUGHT OF
VIVEKANANDA AND AUROBINDO

By Dennis Dalton

THE FULL TITLE of this discussion should be "The Idea of Freedom in the Political Thought of Vivekananda and Aurobindo, as seen through Western Eyes", or, rather, through the eyes of a student of Western political thought. The approach to the subject will be two-fold: first, to understand the idea of freedom as Vivekananda and Aurobindo understood it, through an examination of what they said about freedom and a comparison of their views with some Western thinking on the concept. The second aspect of the approach will consider what light an analysis of this particular idea throws upon the formulation of a general method of analysis for the Western student of Indian social and political thought; that is, for a study of Indian ideas on freedom as well as on related concepts. The central concern, then, lies with the problem of the relevance of Western political thought for Indian ideas, and especially for the Indian idea of freedom. The suggestion is not that an understanding of the Indian idea of freedom must involve comparison with Western thought, or that it demands construction of a method derived from the Western tradition. The point is rather that this two-fold analysis may offer *one way* of approaching a complex body of ideas.

The concept of freedom was selected for several reasons. First, it is found repeatedly in the writings of recent Indian political thinkers; it occupies a crucial place in their political theory. Second, the idea offers fruitful comparisons with aspects of both the Western and the Indian traditions; and, on the basis of these comparisons, an analysis may be made of the effect of the Western impact on Indian political thought: its effect as seen both in the new ideas that it introduced, as well as in the re-statement that it induced of traditional Indian themes. Finally, the idea of freedom offers a significant instance of a well-known tendency in Indian thought noted by the great Indologist, Louis Renou, when he said, "The Indian mind is constantly seeking hidden correspondences between things which belong to entirely distinct conceptual systems."[1] Modern Indian political thought offers few exceptions to Renou's generalization: concepts, here, seldom stand alone; rather they are found with complements. In this sense, an analysis of the idea of freedom, and of the manner in which it complements other themes, throws light upon some larger aspects of Indian political thought. For the idea is invariably seen as a complementary principle: as one side of the coin, the other side completing its very meaning. To describe this as an interrelatedness of concepts is to imply a dualism which does not exist: when Gandhi said "God is Truth and Truth is God", he did not mean that these concepts were interrelated but rather that they were interchangeable. Sir Isaiah Berlin, in his essay *Two Concepts of Liberty*, insists that "Everything is what it is: liberty is liberty, not equality or fairness or justice or human happiness or a quiet conscience".[2] But for most modern Indian political thinkers freedom is identifiable with several other qualities: among them are self-realization, salvation, truth and harmony. The following passage from Aurobindo Ghosh represents both a good working definition of the Indian idea of freedom as well as an indication of the conceptual correspondences that surround it:

"By liberty we mean the freedom to obey the law of our being, to grow to our natural self-fulfilment, to find out naturally and freely our harmony with our environment. The dangers and disadvantages of liberty, the disorder, strife, waste and confusion to which its wrong use leads, are indeed obvious. But they arise from the absence or defect of the sense of unity between individual and individual, between community and community, which pushes them to assert themselves at the expense of each other instead of growing by mutual help and interchange and to assert freedom for themselves in the very act of encroaching on the free development of their fellows. If a real, a spiritual and psychological unit were effecuated, liberty would have no perils and disadvantages; for free individuals enamoured of unity would be compelled by themselves, by their own need, to accommodate perfectly their own growth with the growth of their fellows and would not feel themselves complete except in the free growth of others. Because of our present imperfection and the ignorance of our mind and will, law and regimentation have to be called in to restrain and to compel from

[1] Louis Renou, *Religions of Ancient India* (London, 1955), p. 18
[2] Isaiah Berlin, *Two Concepts of Liberty* (Oxford, 1959), p. 10

outside. The facile advantages of a strong law and compulsion are obvious, but equally great are the disadvantages. Such perfection as it succeeds in creating tends to be mechanical and even the order it imposes turns out to be artificial and liable to break down if the yoke is loosened or the restraining grasp withdrawn. Carried too far, an imposed order discourages the principle of natural growth which is the true method of life and may even slay the capacity for real growth. We repress and overstandardize life at our peril; by over-regimentation we crush Nature's initiative and habit of intuitive self-adaptation. Dwarfed or robbed of elasticity, the devitalized individuality, even while it seems outwardly fair and symmetrical, perishes from within. Better anarchy than the long continuance of a law which is not our own or which our real nature cannot assimilate. And all repressive or preventive law is only a make shift, a substitute for the true law which must develop from within and be not a check on liberty, but its outward image and visible expression. Human society progresses really and vitally in proportion as law becomes the child of freedom; it will reach its perfection when, man having learned to know and become spiritually one with his fellow-man, the spontaneous law of his society exists only as the outward mould of his self-governed inner liberty."[3]

Aurobindo is quite representative of Indian thinking on freedom in his unequivocal individualism, his insistence that perfect freedom is inner freedom, realized only in a spiritual sense, and finally in the close correspondence he draws between liberty and obedience to one's own will. "By liberty", he says, "we mean the freedom to obey our being."

How may a familiarity with Western political thought help one to understand this view of freedom? A first, and a necessary, step that the Western student may take is to examine overt Western influences on particular Indian thinkers. With Aurobindo, such influence is relatively easy to show, for he spent his entire youth in England, and graduated from Cambridge in Western classical studies. He repeatedly expresses his admiration for European thought. Vivekananda, too, freely admits the powerful impact that certain Western writers made upon his life and thought. But while the immediate effect of this impact was to turn Vivekananda and Aurobindo toward the West, the ultimate result was to drive them back into their own tradition, not merely in the spirit of negative reaction, but, at their best, in an

[3] Sri Aurobindo, *The Ideal of Human Unity* (Pondicherry, 1962), pp. 564–6

attempt to incorporate Western ideas into a basically Indian conceptual framework.

Aurobindo wrote about Westernization in India:

"Side by side with this movement and more characteristic and powerful there has been flowing an opposite current. This first started on its way by an integral reaction, a vindication and re-acceptance of everything Indian as it stood and because it was Indian. We have still waves of this impulse and many of its influences continuing among us; for its work is not yet completed. But in reality the reaction marks the beginning of a more subtle assimilation and fusing; for in vindicating ancient things it has been obliged to do so in a way that will at once meet and satisfy the old mentality and the new, the traditional and the critical mind. This in itself involves no mere return, but consciously or unconsciously hastens a restatement. And the riper form of the return has taken as its principle a synthetical restatement; it has sought to arrive at the spirit of the ancient culture and, while respecting its forms and often preserving them to revivify, has yet not hesitated also to remould, to reject the outworn and to admit whatever new motive seemed assimilable to the old spirituality or apt to widen the channel of its larger evolution. Of this freer dealing with past and present, this preservation by reconstruction, Vivekananda was in his life-time the leading exemplar and the most powerful exponent."[4]

"Preservation by reconstruction": this single phrase sums up the essence of the Indian attempt. Some Western Indologists, struck by the radical nature of the reconstruction, neglect the aspect of preservation, and thus seriously underestimate the complexity of modern Indian thought; this endlessly shifting body of ideas, with its continuing transformation of words, symbols and concepts.

The contention, for example, often made by writers on modern India, that the whole of Gandhi's political thought was inspired by Tolstoy, Ruskin and The Sermon on the Mount does point up Gandhi's own important acknowledgment of Western influences; what it ignores is Gandhi's insistence that his main purpose was to assimilate what he considered the highest ideals of the West into a fundamentally Indian outlook. To stress the Western side of Gandhi's thought is only to reiterate a point which Gandhi himself made; but to do this to the exclusion of his equal emphasis upon certain themes of the Indian tradition is simply not to take what he said seriously. And, if there is one bit of naïveté in which the Western student should indulge, it is the belief, at least at the start, that the Indians meant what they said. Indian thought is not merely a reasonable facsimile of certain Western ideas that may be explained upon the basis of Western influences alone. The alternative position is that the Western student should approach Indian thought not in the easy expectation of finding an Asian Tolstoy or Ruskin, but rather with a willingness to grapple with a complex series of conceptual correspondences, emerging largely from a conscious Indian attempt to fuse the ideas of two highly divergent civilizations. In short, the fact of difference must be faced. Yet a method is needed, not only to accommodate difference, but to exploit what similarities there are, that they may lead the Western student to an increased understanding of Indian thought; and that method lies in the construction of conceptual parallels. A discussion of just one of these parallels, between the Indian and the Western views of the idea of freedom, may serve to indicate a single aspect of the type of method envisaged here, as well as to illustrate the complexity of one particular idea of modern Indian thought.

In a consideration of the Indian and Western ideas on freedom, the conception of freedom expressed by Aurobindo above, that is, freedom as obedience to the law of one's being, represents the basis of the Indian idea. However, Vivekananda made an extremely important development which attempted to incorporate the Western idea of political and social liberty into the classical Indian conception of freedom as spiritual liberation or salvation. The crux of this development occurred with the interpretation of freedom not only as a spiritual state, but as the object of a continuing struggle, as a value that was gradually fulfilled through an evolutionary process which rendered the attainment of freedom desirable at all levels of consciousness: political and social as well as moral and spiritual. This development had no precedent in classical Indian thought; ancient India possessed no idea of political or social liberty. Heretofore, realization of spiritual freedom had involved, among other things, leading a pure life, knowledge of the Vedas and devotion to a good *guru*. With the Western impact, the emphasis was changed: attainment of spiritual freedom was now thought to be furthered by social and political liberty, vital stages in a grand quest for complete liberation.

Indians often speak of political freedom as "external" and spiritual freedom as "internal"; this implies a duality, to the Western mind, which is not intended. Their main point is that "internal" freedom complements "external" freedom; the latter, in providing opportunity for growth, contributes to the development of the former; while spiritual freedom, as the culmination of the quest, the highest stage of the process, brings complete self-realization, perception of one's harmony with all being. This close correspondence of internal with external freedom, as well as an acknowledgment of India's indebtedness to the West for the idea of the latter, is expressed well in this passage from Aurobindo. In speaking of the ideals of liberty, equality and fraternity, as they appeared in eighteenth-century French thought, he says:

"Three words have the power of remoulding nations and Governments, liberty, equality and fraternity. These words cast forth into being from the great stir and movement of the eighteenth century continue to act on men because they point to the ultimate goal towards which human evolution ever moves. This liberty to which we progress is liberation out of a state of bondage. We move from a state of bondage to an original liberty. This is what our own religion teaches. This is what our own philosophy suggests as the goal towards which we move, *mukti* or *moksha*. We are bound in the beginning by a lapse from pre-existent freedom, we strive to shake off the bonds, we move forward and forward until we have achieved the ultimate emancipation that utter freedom of the soul, of the body or the whole man, that utter freedom from all bondage towards which humanity is always aspiring. We in India have found a mighty freedom within ourselves, our brother-men in Europe have worked towards freedom without. We have been moving on parallel lines towards the same end. They have found out the way to external freedom. We have found out the way to internal freedom. We meet and give to each other what we have gained. We have learned from them to aspire after external as they will learn from us to aspire after internal freedom."[5]

Vivekananda and Aurobindo, then, extend the Indian tradition to underwrite a value foreign to that tradition; but in the process this value was given traditional support.

Turning to Western thought, we have the immediate problem of making about twenty-five hundred years of thinking about freedom manageable enough to consider here in comparison with modern Indian thought. We might begin by briefly outlining the well-known two concepts of freedom as seen by three modern Western political thinkers: Isaiah Berlin, Maurice Cranston, and Mortimer Adler.

[5] Sri Aurobindo, *Speeches* (Pondicherry, 1922), pp. 93-4

Berlin, in his *Two Concepts of Liberty*, distinguishes between negative and positive freedom. Negative liberty, he says, is simply the area within which a man can do what he wants. Hobbes, Locke, Bentham and Mill are identified with this position. Positive freedom, on the other hand, demands obedience, but obedience to a law which we prescribe to ourselves and to which no man can enslave himself. Kant and Hegel represent this position.[6] In his *Freedom, a New Analysis* Maurice Cranston is in agreement with Berlin's distinction between negative and positive freedom, but further divides the latter category into "rational freedom" as seen by Kant, which is individualistic, finding freedom in self-discipline, and "compulsory rational freedom" as conceived by Hegel which finds freedom in discipline alone, thus becoming a social ethic.[7] Finally, the most exhaustive consideration of the idea of freedom has been made by Mortimer Adler for The Institute for Philosophical Research, an American association. Adler distinguishes between "circumstantial" and "acquired" freedom. Circumstantial freedom "lies in the unhampered actions by which the individual pursues his own good as he sees it and thus realizes his desires". Thus, advocates "look to the circumstances that affect a man's ability to carry out his wishes".[8] Adler identifies this conception of freedom with the positions of Hobbes, Hume, Bentham and Mill. Acquired freedom, according to Alder,

"consists in doing as one ought; it depends on the state of mind or character which enables a man to act in accordance with a moral law, or an ideal befitting human nature. If some authors who attribute acquired freedom to man also take circumstances into account, they do so only with respect to the individual's ability to execute what he wills, not with respect to his ability to will as he ought. The latter ability is in no sense circumstantial. The individual does not have it or lack it merely as a result of living in a favourable or unfavourable environment, but always as a result of developing his own personality, character, or mind in a certain way."

Thus, for Adler, the distinction is between "the acquired freedom of being able to will as one ought, and the circumstantial freedom of being able to do as one pleases".[9] Adler sees acquired freedom represented in Plato, the Stoics, the Church Fathers, Kant, and Hegel.

---

[6] Berlin, op. cit., p. 21 and *passim*
[7] Maurice Cranston, *Freedom, A New Analysis* (London, 1953), pp. 28–9
[8] Mortimer J. Adler, *The Idea of Freedom* (New York, 1958), p. 200
[9] Adler, op. cit., p. 251

If we accept this broad distinction between negative and positive, or circumstantial and acquired freedom, in Western political thought, as I suggest we do for the purposes of this discussion, then we might turn to a consideration of these two concepts of liberty *vis à vis* the modern Indian position. The Indian view of the highest form of freedom, spiritual freedom, is close to what Berlin would call positive freedom, or what Cranston would call rational freedom; it is perhaps closest to Adler's idea of acquired freedom. This immediately raises the question, "Are the Indians really talking about freedom?" Cranston expresses grave doubts that the idea of "rational freedom", as it appears in Kant, really means freedom at all; and he is quite certain that what he calls "compulsory rational freedom" as it appears in Hegel represents a complete distortion of the idea.[10] John Laird, in his book *On Human Freedom*, says: "If we are seriously asked to believe that freedom means self-control under the jurisdiction of right reason, it seems clear without further argument that freedom means no such thing." [11] H. J. Muller, in his study *Freedom in the Ancient World*, rejects explicitly the classical Indian conception of spiritual freedom as totally irrelevant to the whole meaning of freedom.[12] Finally, Berlin appears sceptical throughout his essay of the notion of positive freedom; this scepticism is bluntly expressed in the sentence quoted at the outset of this discussion. We must ask, here, precisely this question: Is spiritual or moral freedom, as, for instance, Kant, or the Indians, see it, really freedom at all?

The second question concerns the attempt of the modern Indian theorists to incorporate the Western idea of social and political liberty into the classical Indian concept of spiritual freedom. Berlin concludes his essay with the argument that advocates of negative freedom insist upon

"absolute barriers to the imposition of one man's will on another's. The freedom of a society is measured by the strength of these barriers, and the number and importance of the paths which they keep open. This is almost at the opposite pole from the purpose of those who believe in liberty in the positive – self-directive – sense. The former want to curb authority as such. The latter want it placed in their own hands. That is the cardinal issue. These are not two different interpretations of a single concept, but two profoundly divergent and irreconcilable attitudes to the ends of life." [13]

[10] Cranston, op. cit.
[11] John Laird, *On Human Freedom* (London, 1947), p. 23
[12] Herbert J. Muller, *Freedom in the Ancient World* (London, 1961), pp. 109–10.
[13] Berlin, op. cit., pp. 51–2

The first thing that the Indians would deny is that negative and positive freedom are two irreconcilable ends or values. It is here that the test of their conceptual correspondences becomes crucial: is this an "either-or" proposition or are these two types of freedom two sides of the same coin? Is this absorption trick that the Indians have attempted to pull off legitimate? And, if so, what parallels does it have in Western political thought?

If these questions illustrate the difficulty of understanding a particular idea, the idea of freedom, in modern Indian thought, the second problem that may be raised here concerns the general approach that may be taken, by a student of Western political thought, toward understanding Indian ideas as they are related to the idea of freedom. Or to put it another way: if the first question to be posed is, "What relevance has Western thinking on the idea of freedom for that idea as it occurs in modern Indian political thought?"; the second question is, "What help can Western thought give in formulating a general method for research into the whole nexus of Indian political ideas of which the idea of freedom is an integral part?"

A methodological beginning may be made with problems which have perennially concerned Western thought: the problems of the nature of man; of the idea of an Absolute, and its relevance to the sphere of politics; of the right relation of the individual to society; of the nature of the good society; and of the way of right action. If one examines a number of contemporary Indian thinkers, one finds that several have concerned themselves with these problems, and that four, Vivekananda, Aurobindo, Gandhi, and Tagore, have conceptualized their responses to a fairly high level (judged, of course, by Western standards). When the next step is taken of selecting the idea of freedom and applying that to Indian thought, one finds that each of these four have made that idea a central principle of their theory, and that there is the closest possible relationship in their thinking between the idea of freedom and the other problems, cited above, which have been historically treated by Western thought. A straightforward example of the correspondences drawn among the three concepts of the nature of man, the belief in an Absolute, and the idea of spiritual freedom appears in this passage from Vivekananda:

"The God of heaven, becomes the God in nature, and the God in nature becomes the God who is nature, and the God who is nature becomes the God within this temple of the body, and the God dwelling in the temple of the body at last becomes the temple itself, becomes the soul and man – and there it reaches the last words it can teach. He whom the sages have been seeking in all these places is in our own hearts; the voice that you heard was right, says the Vedanta, but the direction you gave the voice was wrong. That ideal of freedom that you perceived was correct, but you projected it outside yourself, and that was your mistake. Bring it nearer and nearer, until you find that it was all the time within you, it was the Self of your own self."[14]

The ideas of man's self, of God, and of freedom are seen here as inter-changeable concepts. Freedom is viewed as a spiritual quality, but as it was pointed out earlier, this spiritual concept of freedom became extended in modern Indian thought to embrace the Western ideas of political and social liberty as well. Freedom *from* all bondage, physical and mental, material and psychological, as well as political and social, was seen by the Indians as one side of the coin; freedom *to* perceive one's harmony with all being and to realize one's self was the other side. Conceptual correspondences are made, then, of God with man, of man and God with freedom, and of freedom in the sense of salvation with freedom in the sense of social and political liberty.

The next concern may involve using the method derived from Western thought to gain an understanding of the Indians' thinking on each of these problems, as well as of the conceptual correspondences which they had made among them. A Western thinker who has articulated well the problems of Western thought, and who has a parallel idea of freedom, is Plato and especially the Plato of the *Republic*. By seeing these problems as Plato saw them, examining his responses, analysing the correspondences which he made, it seems that something may be learned about an approach to the study of modern Indian political thought.

The most obvious parallels concern the principles of the right rela-tion of the individual to society and the nature of the good society. Each emphasizes a sense of social duty, rather than a struggle for individual right, in their mutual quest for harmony. The good society rests for each in a stratified system of social functions, the individual perceiving his duty, and performing it in accordance with the dictates of his own soul. Neither Plato nor the Indian thinkers feel that this sense of duty can be inspired or maintained by an external agency; the spirit of justice, for Plato, and of Dharma, for the Indians, must

[14] Swami Vivekananda, *The Complete Works of Swami Vivekananda* (8 vols., Calcutta, 1952), ii. 128

become internalized or instinctive; it must be felt as a law not of the state, but of one's own nature. The whole basis for Plato's views on the individual in society rests with his conceptions of the nature of man and of the existence of an Absolute. Justice becomes internalized within the human soul, to which the Absolute is discernible. The parallel is close to Indian thought, throughout; and, given this agreement on the concepts of man, society, and the Absolute, it is not surprising that for both Plato and the Indians the way of right action is fulfilled in individuals who have achieved spiritual self-realization, and work with a sense of renunciation for the establishment of social harmony.

The *Republic's* concern with the main problem considered here, the idea of freedom, is not as explicit as with some of the others. It was mentioned, before, that Adler considered Plato the first exponent of freedom in the "acquired" sense, but this perhaps needs more explanation. The *Republic* is, above all, a book about justice (its original title, "A Book Concerning Justice"), but the term justice must not be understood in the narrow sense that we use it today. For Plato, justice was synonymous with virtue and goodness; just action meant that a man is doing what he ought to do. The modern conception of justice is different; we think of justice as only one of many possible virtues; we may want a man to be merciful rather than just. Plato, however, would say that if mercy is the right quality of action, then this is just; justice comprehends all action that ought to be done. It is, moreover, a quality of the human soul, the highest state that the soul may attain; when man performs what ought to be done his soul has achieved the right balance, and he is responding to its highest element. And it is in this sense that Plato understands not only the just or the virtuous action, but the free action as well. For, as Ernest Barker says, in his excellent treatment of Plato's political thought, "freedom for Plato means the free action of the whole man according to the will of the best part of his being".[15] This freedom, too, is as the Indians understood it. It is not, however, the idea of freedom alone, but this idea within a nexus of conceptual correspondences, and correspondences among similar concerns, that make the construction of parallels fruitful. The suggestion is not, of course, that the level or content of the Indians' response in any way approached Plato's; but there does appear a similar way of thinking, a way of thinking shared with a certain stream of Western thinkers, but conceptualized most clearly and profoundly by Plato. It must be emphasized finally that the intent, here, has been to

[15] Barker, Ernest, *The Political Thought of Plato and Aristotle* (New York, 1959), p. 187

suggest that parallels may be drawn, that some significant similarities between the Indian and Western traditions do seem to exist. This is not meant, however, to overlook the differences, even though they have not been discussed here. No Western thinker can take us all the way in an understanding of Indian thought. If Plato comes closest, that only means that he is less far away, perhaps, than, say, Hobbes or Bentham.

To summarize: one purpose, here, has been to examine the relevance of Western political theory for modern Indian thought. The essay began by narrowing this study down to one idea, the idea of freedom, as it appears among a half dozen Indian political thinkers of this century. Two main problems have emerged: the first concerns the nature of the concept of freedom itself, and the difficulty of understanding its meaning within the framework of conceptual correspondences that the Indians have drawn. This first problem has been dealt with, here, by indicating very briefly the Western conceptions of negative and positive freedom, and asking what relevance they may have for the Indian idea. One concern lies with the expression of doubt, by so many recent Western political thinkers, that the idea of positive freedom, which is closest to the Indian conception, really means freedom at all. Another concern arises from Berlin's assertion, shared by others, that the two concepts of freedom are irreconcilable; for the Indians, in the face of the Western impact, attempted to incorporate the Western into the classical Indian idea. Indeed, the Indians go so far as to say that negative freedom has no real meaning unless possessed by men who appreciate the highest goal of positive freedom. The second problem raises a broader question, the difficulty of conceiving a method which the student of Western ideas may use in his analysis of Indian thought. The conceptual framework used here has been formed around a half dozen key problems of Western political thought. It appears that there is a parallel way of thinking between the Indians and certain major Western theorists, pre-eminently Plato. A. N. Whitehead once said, "All Western philosophy is a series of footnotes to Plato", and at first glance, perhaps, Indian thought might be seen as included among the notes; but unfortunately it is not that simple: there are highly important differences as well as significant parallels. What is needed is a method that may be employed to analyse both. The concern which unites the two problems outlined here may be expressed in this question on which we may conclude: To what use may the Western student of political thought put his training in a study of some of the main ideas behind the Indian nationalist movement?

NATIONALIST INTERPRETATIONS OF ARTHAŚĀSTRA IN INDIAN HISTORICAL WRITING[1]

By Johannes H. Voigt

THE HISTORY OF modern Indian historical writing is the history of the adoption of European methods and the emancipation from European ideas – i.e. of non-Indian views, aspects, standards and judgments – and the creation of an Indian concept of India's past. The full impact of the *Arthaśāstra* upon modern Indian historical writing can best be measured by casting a glance upon some earlier European concepts of India, which had to a large extent been accepted by Indians in the nineteenth and early twentieth centuries, either silently or explicitly. European concepts of India, especially of Ancient India, were a series of clichés, so tenacious of life that even the considerable "re-discovery" of Indian history in the course of the nineteenth century by the hard and meticulous work of philologists and archaeologists was not sufficient to kill them entirely.

In nineteenth-century European works on India, two different, in fact opposite, tendencies of interpretation of Indian history can be distinguished, the one romantic and glorifying, the other rationalistic and utilitarian, giving respectively a positive or negative evaluation of India's past.

The former as expressed in the works of William Jones, the brothers Schlegel, and Max Müller – to name only a few – is, however, no more than a modern, scientifically supported, but still emotionally charged, version of the concept of the wonderland of India which had dominated the minds of Europeans in the ancient past as well as in the Middle Ages.

The second tendency, with its negative and critical evaluation of

[1] I am greatly indebted to Dr. K. A. Ballhatchet for his suggestions on the final wording of this paper, which was read at his Indian Seminar on 19 November 1964. A modified German version will be published under the title "Arthaśāstra – Interpretationen in der nationalistischen Geschichtsschreibung Indiens" in the journal *Geschichte in Wissenschaft und Unterricht*

India, received a powerful impetus from evangelical and missionary writings as well as from the philosophy of Utilitarianism at the beginning of the nineteenth century.[2] The ideas, not only of the preceding period of Enlightenment, but also of the Middle Ages and even of Ancient Europe, can be easily recognized as harbingers of this tendency also.

European clichés about India were handed down from generation to generation; because of the limited knowledge of India's past, they served as logical, if not philosophical, bridges or interpolations of the few known facts, and appeared so convincing – a result of their constant repetition and uncritical acceptance by European thinkers in the nineteenth century – that even Indians could not escape their spell and accepted them as final verdicts.

These were the most deeply rooted generalizations concerning India's history:

(1) From the strong conservatism and the adherence of Indians to tradition and the lack of indigenous historical writing in the past it was concluded that India never had had a past that could justifiably be called "history".[3]

(2) From the ancient Indians' lack of a sense of history, it was concluded that India had never been a nation. She had spent all her energy in metaphysical speculations.[4]

[2] Cp. K. A. Ballhatchet, "Some Aspects of Historical Writing on India by Protestant Missionaries during the Nineteenth and Twentieth Centuries", in: *Historians of India, Pakistan and Ceylon*, ed. by C. H. Philips (London, 1961), pp. 344–53. Also J. H. Voigt, "England und Indien 1784–1858", in *Geschichte in Wissenschaft und Unterricht* (November 1963), p. 718, and S. N. Mukherjee "Sir William Jones and the British Attitudes towards India", *J.R.A.S.* parts 1 and 2 (1964), pp. 37–47

[3] Leopold v. Ranke, for instance, excluded India (and China) from his concept of a universal history with the following argument: "Ihr Altertum ist fabelhaft. Ihr Zustand gehört mehr der Naturgeschichte"; from his *Idee der Universalhistorie* (1831?), quoted by E. Kessel, "Ranke's Idee der Universalhistorie", in *Historische Zeitschrift*, vol. 178 (1954), p. 303

[4] The most frequently referred to judgment is that of Friedrich Max Müller, published in 1859: "The Hindus were a nation of philosophers . . . But, taken as a whole, history supplies no second instance, where the inward life of the soul has completely absorbed all the practical faculties of the whole people, and, in fact, almost destroyed those faculties by which a nation gains its place in history. It might therefore be justly said that India has no place in the political history of the world" (*A History of Sanskrit Literature*, London, 1859, p. 31). Max Müller's view was not at all original. It was at his time already a cliché, which owed its widespread acceptance no doubt to Hegel's identification of "actual" history and "written" history and his pointed conclusion on India: "Bei einem solchen Volke

(3) India had never shown any signs of development. Her society had been stagnant, and her polity had, since time immemorial, been an "Oriental" or "Asiatic" despotism.[5] The discovery of the *Arthaśāstra* and its partial publication in 1905 in *The Indian Antiquary* by R. Shamasastry[6] was an "ancient contribution" of some political significance to the then heated discussion on the Revenue and Land Policy of the British. In the academic field, it caused a sensation of the greatest magnitude. With it, many old cherished clichés about Indian history lost much of their power of conviction. The *Arthaśāstra*, in fact, brought about a revolution in Indian historical writing and provided a historical support for the Indian National Movement, which was not left unchallenged by English historians.

The title *Arthaśāstra*[7] is a compound of the terms *artha* (material

---

ist denn das, was wir im doppelten Sinne *Geschichte* heissen, nicht zu suchen . . . Weil die Inder keine Geschichte, als Historie, haben um deswillen haben sie keine Geschichte als Taten (res gestae), d.i. keine Herausbildung zu einem wahrhaft politischen Zustande" (quoted from G. W. F. Hegel's *Vorlesungen über die Philosophie der Geschichte* (edition of F. Brunstäd), Stuttgart, 1961, pp. 241 and 243)

[5] Karl Marx wrote in the *New York Daily Tribune* in 1853: "Indian society has no history at all, at least no known history. What we call its history, is but the history of the successive intruders who founded their empire on the passive basis of that unresisting and unchanging society." (Quoted from Karl Marx and Friedrich Engels, *The First Indian War of Independence 1857–1859*, Moscow, 1959, p. 32.). Cp. K. D. Erdmann, "Die asiatische Welt im Denken von Karl Marx und Friedrich Engels", in *Historische Forschungen und Probleme*, Festschrift for Peter Rassow, edited by K. E. Born (Wiesbaden, 1961), pp. 256–83. Hegel denied India any historical development: "Das Sichverbreiten des Indischen ist vorgeschichtlich, *denn Geschichte ist nur das, was in der Entwicklung des Geistes eine wesentliche Epoche ausmacht*. Das Hinausgehen Indiens überhaupt ist nur eine stumme, tatlose Verbreitung, d.h. ohne politische Handlung" (quoted from Hegel, op. cit., p. 215). On despotism, he chose the strongest possible terms: "In Indien ist daher der willkürlichste, schlechteste, entehrendste Despotism zu Hause" (ibid., p. 241). On Hegel's concept of India, cp. F. Glasenapp, *Das Indienbild deutscher Denker* (Stuttgart, 1960), pp. 39–60

[6] R. Shamasastry, "Chanakya's Land and Revenue Policy", in *The Indian Antiquary*, vol. xxiv (1905), pp. 5 ff. and 110 ff.

[7] *Arthaśāstra* was published in its complete text for the first time by R. Shamasastry in the *Bibliotheca Sanskrita*, vol. 37, Mysore, 1909. The first translation into English was published by Shamasastry under the title *Kauṭilya's Arthaśāstra*, Mysore, 1915, the 6th edition of which was published in 1960. The most recent critical edition and translation into English was prepared by R. P. Kangle, *The Kauṭiliya Arthaśāstra*: part i: A Critical Edition with a Glossary, Bombay, 1960; part ii: An English Translation with Critical and Explanatory Notes, Bombay, 1963

gain) and *śāstra* (treatise or science), meaning "the treatise of material gain."[8] *Arthaśāstra* has been attributed to Kauṭilya, also known as *Chanakya*, who was the Minister under Chandragupta Maurya (*c.* 322–298 B.C.).[9] Kauṭilya does not claim entire originality for all the ideas and opinions expressed. On the contrary, as was the custom in India, he refers explicitly to the teachings of former *gurus*, of whom he mentions among others the names of Śukra and Brihaspati. He begins his treatise with the words: "Devotion to Śukra and Brihaspati! All the different *arthaśāstras*, which, in view of the conquest and rule of the earth, have been composed by ancient teachers, are in the main put together here, and form this one *arthaśāstra*." [10]

The fifteen chapters (or "books" as they are called) deal with education and science, the qualities of a king (ruler), the political espionage system (1), the revenue and financial system of the state (2), the civil and criminal law (3 and 4), the means of strengthening the power of the state (5), sovereignty and the extension of rule (6), the six ways and means of conducting foreign policy, i.e. peace, war, neutrality, alliance, peace-treaty and declaration of war (7), the calamities of the elements of sovereignty (8), preparations for an attack (9), the battle (10), the co-operation with corporations (11), the means of policy to be used against a superior enemy (12), the strategy of conquering fortresses (13), the political use of spiritual and chemical

---

[8] Cp. *Arthaśāstra*, book xv, ch. i, 1st sentence

[9] The question of Kauṭilya's authorship has been the subject of a very long but not yet finally decided controversy. The strongest arguments against an origin of *Arthaśāstra* in the fourth century B.C. were brought forward by Julius Jolly's "Kollektaneen zum Kauṭiliya Arthaśāstra", in *Nachrichten von der k. Gesellschaft der Wissenschaften zu Göttingen* (1916), pp. 348ff. Hermann Jacobi, on the other hand, arrived at the conclusion that Kauṭilya was the author: "Zur Frühgeschichte der indischen Philosophie", in *Sitzungsberichte der k. preuss. Akademie der Wissenschaften* (Berlin, 1911), p. 743. A recent confirmation of Jacobi's thesis was given by Friedrich Wilhelm: "Die Zitate in Kauṭalya's Arthasastra", in *Akten des vierundzwanzigsten Orientalistenkongresses* München 28. Aug. bis 4. Sept. 1957, edited by H. Franke (Wiesbaden, 1959), pp. 579–82. Cp. F. Wilhelm, *Politische Polemiken im Staatslehrbuch des Arthasastra*, Wiesbaden, 1960. A. L. Basham, on the other hand, rejects the idea of Kauṭilya's authorship, although he admits that *Arthaśāstra* might have as its source an earlier but lost work by Kautilya: see Basham, *The Wonder that was India* (New York, 1955), pp. 50 and 79. Cp. also Romila Thapar: "The Date of Arthaśāstra", in *Aśoka and the Decline of the Mauryas* (Oxford, 1961), pp. 218–25, and H. C. Raychaudhuri, "Note on the date of Arthaśāstra", in *The History and Culture of the Indian People: The Age of Imperial Unity*, ed. by R. C. Majumdar (Bombay, 1953), pp. 285–7

[10] After J. J. Meyer, *Das Altindische Buch vom Welt-und Staatsleben. Das Arthaçāstra des Kauṭilya* (Leipzig, 1926), p. 1

D

means, like medicine and *mantras* (14), and finally with the principles of the composition of *Arthaśāstra* and how the author wishes the work to be understood (15).

It has become a commonplace in the literature on *Arthaśāstra* and ancient Indian polity to compare this ancient Indian text with Machiavelli's *Il Principe*. As far as the scrupulousness of the prescribed means of politics is concerned, neither bears the palm; they are equals.[11] There is, however, a great difference between *Arthaśāstra* and *Il Principe* in two respects. They differ, first, in the scope of their teachings: Machiavelli is only concerned with the means of politics, the maintenance of rule and foreign policy, whereas Kauṭilya devotes much space to what one may call home policy, economic policy, the judicial system, and military strategy, besides the conduct of foreign policy. The two works differ secondly in the choice of arguments that are to support the lessons. Machiavelli refers frequently to historical events to confirm his views; Kauṭilya, on the other hand, abstracts his teachings entirely from actual history and rejects opposite older views in a polemic way. As Friedrich Wilhelm wrote, *Arthaśāstra* is a typical *śāstra*, the methods of which are argumentation and deduction with the aim of generalizing from any single case and event.[12]

The discovery of *Arthaśāstra* startled the Indologists, epigraphists, and archaeologists, who were conducting painstaking detailed philological and archaeological research by which they hoped to "reconstruct" the "lost", or rather "not transmitted", Indian history. Here now was a text which struck at the root of the current and never contested idea that in Ancient India the leading spirits had exclusively been devoted to religious interests and metaphysical speculations.[13]

[11] Kauṭilya, for instance, suggests defeating a superior enemy by killing him at a place of religious devotion during his worship either with stones dropped on him in the interior of the temple or with weapons hidden in the idol and fired from there: *Arthaśāstra*, book xii, ch. 5. Machiavelli formulated advice perhaps less vivid, but not less drastic: "Circumstances may compel a ruler, particularly one recently established, for the preservation of his state to act against the principles which men call good, to break his word, to be ruthless, tyrannical and an enemy of religion." (*The Ruler*. A new translation by Peter Rodd, London, 1954, p. 92.)

[12] Friedrich Wilhelm, *Politische Polemiken*, p. 148; also in "Die Entdeckung der indischen Geschichte" in *Saeculum*, vol. 15 (1964), p. 33

[13] The European cliché of a complete absorption of the Indian intellect in metaphysical speculations died a slow death even in India. In 1907, R. P. Karkaria wrote: "The bias of the Indian mind is certainly not historical. It is metaphysical; it is imaginative . . ." *The Scientific Study of Mahratha History* (Bombay, 1907), p. 4

Arthaśāstra was powerful proof that two thousand and more years ago Indians had been concerned with politics in action and theory. The principles of politics of the ancient past showed indeed a remarkable "this-worldliness" and a *raison d'état* which could not be surpassed by Machiavelli in its lack of religious and ethical scruples.

The outstanding importance that is given to *Arthaśāstra* in modern Indian historical writings is not a little due to the coincidence of its discovery and partial publication with the radicalization of the Indian National Movement in 1905. Ancient Indian history had provided the ideological ammunition with which British justifications of a patriarchal and stern rule over an "ever a-political" India could be shattered and rejected. Now the discovery of politics in Ancient India gave Indian nationalists a strong confidence in their cause; India had not been second to and entirely different from Europe in her past, as had been maintained and believed before. Her greatness need not be sought only in the height of ancient metaphysical thought; it could be found in her political achievements as well.

Since the beginning of this century (more precisely, in its second decade) Indian historians, archaeologists and philologists have no longer been concerned to contradict European interpretations of Indian history by subtle and hair-splitting arguments on problems of detail. It has been no longer this or that interpretation and judgment that mattered, but the concept of Indian history as a whole. In this process of the emancipation of Indian historical writing *Arthaśāstra* was to play a very important role. During the period from 1910 to 1930 there was no Indian historian of renown who did not contribute to the literature on *Arthaśāstra* and Ancient Indian politics in one way or another.

Over the course of the period from 1910 to 1930 different prevailing trends of interpretation are recognizable, which may be described in character, though very unsatisfactorily, as "conservative", "political" and "ideological" trends, each of which dominated the writings on Ancient Indian history for some time. It is very surprising, and not totally explicable, that after 1930 the flood of literature on *Arthaśāstra* came to an almost abrupt end, although none of the works on Ancient India written after 1930 could bypass it. It seems justifiable, therefore, to cast a brief glance also on the post-1930 interpretations of *Arthaśāstra* and Ancient Indian politics. Thus, it is hoped, the changes in the contemporary relevance of the subject can be recognized.

With regard to time and importance, priority must be given to Kashi Prasad Jayaswal, who broke the spell of the sterile accepted interpretations of Ancient India with his epoch-making talk in 1912 on the platform of the third Conference on Hindi Literature in Calcutta. His provocative views, enshrined under the very unassuming title "Introduction to Hindu Polity", reached not only a large number of listeners, but readers all over India by its publication in *The Modern Review* in 1913.[14] Jayaswal contested the romantic, idealized concept of the purely metaphysical inclinations of Indians in the past by attributing a higher value to the political institutions of Ancient India than had hitherto been attributed to the speculative achievements.[15]

He painted a very enticing image of the state in Ancient India: the state had been, according to *Arthaśāstra*, a constitutional monarchy, in which the king had been no more than a figure-head, with the executive in the hands of a ministerial council, and the judiciary functioning independently of the administration.[16] The dominating position of the law was in Jayaswal's eyes a primary characteristic of the state in Ancient India.[17]

Jayaswal did not miss the opportunity to draw a parallel between Indian and European conditions, which encouraged him to the conclusion that feudalism had never existed in India and that there had never been a struggle between ruler and subjects like those known from "despotic and medieval Europe".[18] It is quite obvious that the model after which Jayaswal framed his concept of the ancient Indian state was the constitutional monarchy of Britain. He did not in the least hide his admiration for British constitutional achievements, when he exclaimed: "What a coincidence that the race who evolved the greatest constitutional principles in antiquity should be placed today in contact with the greatest constitutional polity of modern times." [19]

Jayaswal's message to his listeners and readers was that the development of constitutional government was not the monopoly of one nation (meaning the English),[20] and that "the Golden Age" of India's "polity lies not in the past but in the Future".[21]

A more traditional line of interpretation was followed by Narendra Nath Law, who in his studies of *Arthaśāstra* found confirmation of the old view that the rulers in Ancient India had been deified.[22] The ancient machinery of administration roused his admiration: it was

[14] *The Modern Review*, vol. 13 (1913), pp. 535–41, 664–8, and vol. 14 (1913), pp. 77–83, 201–6, 288–91

[15] Ibid., vol. 13, p. 535   [16] Ibid., vol. 14, pp. 81 and 202

[17] Ibid., vol. 14, p. 289   [18] Ibid., vol. 14, p. 290

[19] Ibid., vol. 14, p. 291   [20] Ibid., vol. 14, p. 291

[21] Ibid., vol. 14, p. 290

[22] N. N. Law, "The Religious Aspects of Ancient Hindu Polity", in *The Modern Review*, vol. 22 (1917), pp. 620 f.

aimed at the welfare of the people and it had to cope with an area much bigger than that of British India.[23] This, indeed, implied a subtle criticism of contemporary British rule: why should what was possible in ancient times even under indigenous rule not be possible today?

British India as an ideal loomed large in the views of Pramathanath Banerjea, who wrote a Ph.D. thesis in London on "Public Administration in Ancient India" (1916). The Empire of Chandragupta Maurya was so governed that the home-province was under the direct administration of the central executive, whereas the provinces were governed by viceroys and governors, who were appointed and posted there by the central government.[24] The Vedic popular assemblies had gradually lost their political importance under the constantly encroaching royal authority, so that finally they came to be replaced by the "Great Council" and the "Privy Council".[25] Banerjea held Kauṭilya to be in intellectual respects far superior to Machiavelli, and in political ability equal to Bismarck.[26]

These early interpretations of *Arthaśāstra* may be called "conservative" with regard to the ideals that were read into and discovered in the ancient Indian polity. The example that loomed large in these interpretations was clearly that of the British Empire. The tendency to compare Indian institutions with European and to find them equal or superior[27] – a very understandable reaction to the European superiority-complex and obsession with the unique greatness of ancient Greece and Rome – is very obvious in these early *Arthaśāstra* interpretations. Yet the choice of subject and the reference to India's present and future were revolutionary. One may describe the basis of these interpretations as a "dialectical switch": whereas Indian historians had hitherto lamented their country's fallen state and praised Providence for putting it into the hands of the British, they now read back the cherished ideals of British politics into their own ancient history. By this method satisfaction could be derived from indigenous achievements instead of consolation from the fortune of being under the rule of a foreign, though politically advanced, nation.

When, at the end of the First World War, the agitated discussions

[23] N. N. Law, *Studies in Ancient Hindu Polity* (New York, 1914), p. 68
[24] Pramathanath Banerjea, *Public Administration in Ancient India* (London, 1916), p. 49
[25] Ibid., p. 97   [26] Ibid., p. 11
[27] This tendency is very marked with Rajendralal Mitra, who fought against the obsession of European historians with Greek influences by claiming Indian originality of early art in India; see R. Mitra, *The Antiquities of Orissa*, 2 vols. (Calcutta, 1875 and 1880), and *Buddha Gaya* (Calcutta, 1878)

of the Montagu–Chelmsford proposals came to preoccupy political minds, a real rush of historians to the subject of the ancient Indian constitution set in. The dangers that threatened historical writing, when stimulated by questions of the day and made use of by politicians who were less interested in the past than in the present and future, were appreciated by different men. Already in 1916 K. V. Rangaswami Aiyangar had warned that in India historical issues were "being obscured and findings vitiated by the tendency to treat history as the ally of dogma, and to look into the armoury of our ancient polity for weapons to be used in the arena of modern political controversies".[28] It was, however, difficult for Indian historians to remain indifferent, particularly when historians of the other camp were interpreting Indian history in such a way as to see in the establishment of British rule and its maintenance a historical inevitability and a political, if not humanitarian, necessity.

In the course of its establishment, British rule had first been justified in English (and Indian) writings as a result of "Divine Providence", then as humanitarian obligation – for example, by Macaulay, James Mill, Kaye, Seeley, and others – and finally, at the turn of the century, by arguments drawn from Indian history. This was a consequence of the continual process of the destruction of myths, and of a growing historicism in Imperialist thinking. The "New Imperialism", developing in the last decades of the nineteenth century, based its ideological "superstructure" upon history. W. W. Hunter, V. A. Smith and E. J. Rapson may be regarded as representatives of "imperialist" historical writing on India, and Lord Curzon as a representative of the historically based imperialism. This is evident in Lord Curzon's constant stress on his position in Indian history as being in the line of great Indian rulers, Akbar and Shah Jehan, and in his attempt to emphasize this historical continuity of rule in India by the establishment of the Victoria Memorial Hall in Calcutta. Hunter's "Rulers of India" series included both Indian and British statesmen in India. The penetration of imperialist thought into historical writing is quite obvious in Rapson's *Ancient India*, published in 1914, in which the author maintains:

> "Another lesson which is enforced by the history of the Maurya Empire is that the maintenance of peace, and of those conditions which are essential to progress, depends in India on the *existence of a strong imperial power*. On the downfall of the Maurya Empire, as on

[28] K. V. Rangaswami Aiyangar, *Considerations on Some Aspects of Ancient Indian Polity* (Madras, 1916), p. 3

the downfall of the Mughal Empire, nearly 2000 years later, the individual states which had been peacefully united under the *imperial sway* regained their independence, and the struggle began anew." [29]

In other words, the professed mission to maintain peace in India was justified by reference to history.

The interconnection between imperialist thought and historical writing is well marked in the writings of Vincent A. Smith, the famous author of *The Early History of India* (1904) and *The Oxford History of India* (1919). It must have had an offensive ring in Indian ears, when, just after the termination of the First World War, Indians were told, as one of the parallels between the governments of the Mauryan Empire and of Imperial Germany, that both were supposed to have been founded on a secret service: "The King [as described in Artha-śāstra] employed hosts of spies and detectives masquerading in disguises of all kinds, who were controlled by an espionage bureau as in modern Germany." [30]

The aim of Smith's polemic work, *Indian Constitutional Reform viewed in the Light of History* (1919), was to warn against the delegation of political rights to Indians as was suggested by the Montagu–Chelmsford proposals.[31] In Indian history Smith saw an uninterrupted chain of absolutist rule from the ancient past down to the Moslem and British periods, in which any monarch was able to rule free from the trammels of law, and in such a way could exercise severe justice.[32] Thus Kauṭilya had been nothing but an early theoretician of absolutist monarchical power. The lessons which Smith drew from Indian history were: (1) that the necessary co-operation between the fully developed British democracy and the Indian nations could be best achieved by the Golden Link of the Crown;[33] (2) there could be no Home Rule in the sense of a government by the majority, meaning in India "Hindu-rule".[34]

Smith's historical justification of a monarchical absolutism and the direct rule of the Crown meant a rejection of the proposal to develop representative institutions in India. This was fuel on the flames of the

[29] E. J. Rapson, *Ancient India* (Cambridge, 1914), p. 113. My italics
[30] V. A. Smith, *The Oxford History of India* (Oxford, 1919), p. 89
[31] Cp. A. L. Basham, "Modern Historians of Ancient India", in *Historians of India, Pakistan and Ceylon*, p. 267
[32] V. A. Smith, *Indian Constitutional Reform*, pp. 19 ff.
[33] Ibid., p. 23   [34] Ibid., p. 91

national feelings of Indians and the starting signal for a flood of historical literature intended to prove India's capability for self-government and democracy.[35]

R. C. Majumdar in his *Corporate Life in Ancient India* (1918) countered the imperialist thesis of a constantly "a-political" or "un-political" India with the antithesis that a constitutional monarchy had already been known in Ancient India, expressing itself during election campaigns conducted in the most democratic manner.[36] The executive of the ancient Indian state had developed along the lines of the British in later times.[37] Kauṭilya's imperialism had failed to do away with the centres of corporate life.

Similar to this was the interpretation by Radha Kumud Mookerji, who, in his *Local Government in Ancient India* (1919), proclaimed his conviction that democratic institutions existed during the whole course of Indian history and had not been destroyed by the imperialist system of the Maurya Empire, which had tolerated and recognized local autonomy at the expense of the authority of the central government. Mookerji built a bridge between past and present, history and politics, when he maintained: "Local self-government in ancient India, besides its historical interest, is also of an eminently practical interest." [38] Equally direct and emphatic was his wish that the lessons of Indian history should be useful not only to the Indian people but to the government as well![39]

Benoy Kumar Sarkar conducted in his speeches and writings a vehement crusade against European clichés about India, such as the concept of "Asiatic despotism". But he also condemned the tendency of Indian nationalists, "who try to demonstrate the existence of every modern democratic theory and republican institution and perhaps also of soviet communism in the experience of ancient and medieval Asia".[40] Yet he fell into the very pitfalls which he had warned against, by calling Kauṭilya a "Hindu-Bismarck", who had smashed with "blood and iron" the minor states which stood in the way of an all-

---

[35] A purely political rejection of Smith's thesis was Sir Sankaran Nair's "Minute of Dissent to the Government of India's Despatch of March 5, 1919", in *The Indian Review*, vol. 20 (July 1919), pp. 465–82

[36] R. C. Majumdar, *Corporate Life in Ancient India* (Calcutta, 1918), p. 18

[37] Ibid., p. 53

[38] R. K. Mookerji, *Local Government in Ancient India* (Oxford, 1919), p. 20

[39] Ibid., p. 21

[40] B. K. Sarkar, *The Political Institutions and Theories of the Hindus. A study of Comparative Politics* (Leipzig, 1922), p. 8

Indian nationalism.[41] Sarkar was unable to discover any similarity between Kauṭilya's state and the British Empire; but he found striking resemblances between it and the German Empire, created by Bismarck, particularly in the sphere of state socialism.[42] *Arthaśāstra* was for Sarkar the "bible of imperialism",[43] and the state, as described by Kauṭilya, was of a completely secularized character.[44]

U. N. Ghoshal did not share this opinion. In *Arthaśāstra* the authority of the king was, in his opinion, derived from the Highest Being, although this did not establish a "Divine Right of the King", as was maintained by European writers.[45] Ghoshal was less interested in discovering a certain theory, workable in the present, than in giving a detached analysis of the ideas expounded in the ancient text.[46]

The interpretations of Majumdar and Mookerji, in spite of their apparent differences, have something in common. Both regarded the Arthaśāstran state as an Empire, its foreign politics as imperialistic, and its internal structure as federal – a structure occasionally described as powerless but generally as very tolerant towards autonomous and democratic institutions, like corporations, guilds, and local rule. Sarkar saw in the state in *Arthaśāstra* an embodiment of the combination of power and legality. He coined for it the term *dharmastaaten*, a combination of the Sanskrit term *dharma* and the German word for state, meaning by it what is called in German *Rechtsstaat*.[47] Ghoshal did not deny the authoritarian character of the state. All these interpretations are directly opposed to the theory of Jayaswal, who, during these years, took to the pen at different times in order to develop and confirm his views as expressed *in nuce* in 1912. He gave shape to his theory of a full-fledged constitutional monarchy during the time of Chandragupta Maurya and Kauṭilya by maintaining that all questions of political importance had been discussed in the two houses of the

[41] B. K. Sarkar, "Democratic Ideals and Republican Institutions in India", in *The American Political Science Review*, vol. 12 (1918), p. 591

[42] Sarkar, *The Political Institutions*, p. 173

[43] Sarkar, "Democratic Ideals . . .", loc. cit., p. 585

[44] Sarkar, *The Political Institutions*, p. 13

[45] U. N. Ghoshal, *A History of Political Theories from the Earliest Times to the End of the First Quarter of the Seventeenth Century* A.D. (London, etc., 1923), p. 271

[46] Ghoshal developed his ideas on the subject and published "Some Current Views of the Origin and Nature of Hindu Kingship considered" as Essay No. 4 in *The Beginning of Indian Historiography and Other Essays* (Calcutta, 1944), pp. 104–42

[47] Sarkar, *The Political Institutions*, p. 173

Parliament, called *paura-janapada*, which had been a powerful instrument to curb and control the authority of the king.[48] Jayaswal did not think that the king had been the proprietor of the soil. This is a very important point, as the idea of royal proprietorship of the soil had been closely linked with the idea of absolute rule.[49]

Jayaswal's theory of an ancient constitutional monarchy in India received the greatest popular support compared with the political effect of other historical writings on the subject at the time. His book *Hindu Polity* (1924) became the "Bible for Indian Nationalists".[50]

The immediate post-war period in India was marked by political agitations demanding national independence, an aim that up to that time had been regarded by most nationalists as a very distant, and for all practical purposes, too remote a possibility. With the newly professed aim of complete self-government, ideas and plans of the future structure of the Indian state became of the greatest importance. After the middle of the twenties, one can notice a diminishing concern with a historical legitimization of the constitutional and democratic maturity of India: these ideas and efforts had by then become commonplace in the political parlance of the day. Instead, the nationalists focused their eyes on the problem of the inner structure of India, its social and economic system.

Like B. K. Sarkar, who was attracted by the idea of a centralized state, Hemchandra Ray directed his attention to the social and economic policy as described by Kauṭilya. He detected elements of state socialism of a modern kind that resembled those developed in Germany by the social legislation of Bismarck.[51] The state legislation in *Arthaśāstra* embraced all types of production, from agriculture to mining, and from the regulation of foreign and internal trade to the protection of

[48] K. P. Jayaswal, "The Hindu Parliament under Hindu Monarchy", in *The Modern Review*, vol. 27 (1920), pp. 125 and 133. This essay is part of the later published *Hindu Polity*, Calcutta, 1924

[49] A. L. Basham ("Modern Historians of Ancient India", loc. cit., p. 283) does not think that Jayaswal's rejection of the idea of royal ownership of the soil was a successful proof of his thesis of the existence of a Parliamentary system in Ancient India

[50] Ram Sharan Sharma, *Aspects of Political Ideas and Institutions in Ancient India*, (Delhi, etc., 1959), p. 5

[51] Hemchandra Ray, "Was State-Socialism known in Ancient India? (A Study in Kauṭilya's Arthasastra)", in *Sir Asutosh Mookerjee Silver Jubilee Volumes*, vol. iii, Orientalia part i (Calcutta, 1922), pp. 429–46. Also by the same, "Economic Policy and Functions of the Kauṭilyan State (with Special Reference to the Agents of Production)", in *Journal of the Department of Letters*, Calcutta University, vol. 13 (1926), p. 2 (of this article)

labour against exploitation.[52] The welfare of his nation meant more to the ancient Indian king than his own personal well-being, for, as had been the case with the rulers of Prussia, tradition and duty outweighed all other considerations.[53]

The concern of the state with the promotion of the people's welfare in the economic, social and intellectual spheres, to an extent which no nation of modern Asia or medieval Europe could stand comparison with, was praised by D. R. Bhandarkar as the main feature of ancient Indian politics, when he gave a series of lectures in 1925 at the Banaras Hindu University.[54] He was, however, fully aware that his admiration of the ancient Indian state might carry him too far, for which reason he apologized to his audience: "And one may be pardoned if he feels tempted to see these up-to-date ideas of the modern economic world in the Ancient India of the fourth century B.C., which seems to resemble it in some striking particulars."[55]

Two years later, when Rao Bahadur Rangaswami Aiyangar mounted the platform of the Banaras Hindu University, the main interest in *Arthaśāstra* research had shifted entirely from constitutional history to economic and social problems. Aiyangar was hopeful that the study of such problems in Ancient India would bring about the destruction of the illusion that economic thought was of recent and European origin only.[56] An economic and social study of Ancient India, he believed, might be useful for the solution of present-day problems of the same kind.[57] For the economic and social ideal which Aiyangar saw proclaimed in *Arthaśāstra* was a combination of state socialism and a *laissez-faire* policy. State interference never meant a restriction of personal freedom; on the contrary, it went hand in hand with an increase of personal liberty and rights.[58] The excesses of Western slave-trade and economy had never occurred in Ancient India.[59] In fact, Kauṭilya with his economic theory had guarded against all the possible

[52] Hemchandra Ray, "Economic Policy . . ." loc. cit., pp. 5–18

[53] Ibid., pp. 28 f. Less flattering for German eyes is his comparison of the ancient Indian with the German internal espionage system, which he, like V. A Smith, thought had been developed between 1871 and 1918 in the German Reich; ibid., p. 29

[54] D. R. Bhandarkar, *Some Aspects of Ancient Hindu Polity* (The Manindra Chandra Nandy Lectures 1925) (Benares, 1928), p. 192

[55] Ibid., p. 194

[56] Rao Bahadur Rangaswami Aiyangar, *Aspects of Ancient Indian Economic Thought* (Manindra Chandra Nandy Lectures 1927, Benares Hindu University) (Benares, 1934), p. 5

[57] Ibid., p. 2   [58] Ibid., p. 30   [59] Ibid., p. 55

mistakes that were made in European economic thought and practice.[60] A study and knowledge of ancient Indian economic thought was in Aiyangar's view the best means to ward off the modern Indian tendency to import socialistic ideas that had their origin in the West.[61]

Beni Prasad evaluated *Arthaśāstra* exclusively as a treatise on economic theory.[62] In his book *Theory and Government in Ancient India* (1927), he held that Kauṭilya, despite his monarchical outlook, did not proclaim a despotic form of rule, as in the foreground of his activity stood his professed duty to provide security and welfare for his people.[63] Local peculiarities were respected, and even in the case of conquest of foreign territory, the ruler's duty had always been to respect the individuality and even the dynasty of that territory, and never to force a unitary rule upon its inhabitants.[64]

The shift of scholarly interest from the political and constitutional aspects to the economic and social structure of the ancient Indian state was certainly much determined by the growing importance of research in the economic and social history of Ancient Europe.[65] Still, the changing climate in the sphere of nationalist politics in India was at least as powerful a stimulus for the shift of interests. Ideologies, like socialism and communism, came to be superimposed on Indian nationalism. This ideological impact is quite noticeable in historical writings on Ancient India.

Radha Kumud Mookerji's lectures on *Arthaśāstra*, which he gave in Madras in 1940–41,[66] reflect the influence of an ideology when he, for instance, discovered in Kauṭilya's policy a considerable tendency towards socialism and nationalization in the organization of industry.[67]

What was mere theory and pure reflection before 1947 became a matter of practical policy and of the greatest immediate concern after independence. Economic and social change became the most pressing and difficult problems of Indian politics. It is hardly surprising,therefore, to find that recent interpretations of *Arthaśāstra* reflect the new political

[60] *Aspects of Ancient Indian Economic Thought*, p. 149   [61] Ibid., p. 152
[62] Beni Prasad, *Theory and Government in Ancient India* (Ph.D. thesis London) (Allahabad, 1927), p. 5
[63] Ibid., p. 95   [64] Ibid., p. 146
[65] See for instance. E. Meyer, *Die wirtschaftliche Entwicklung des Altertums*, 2nd ed. 1924, and M. Rostovtzeff, *Gesellschaft und Wirtschaft im römischen Kaiserreich*, 1930
[66] Radha Kumud Mookerji, *Chandragupta Maurya and His Times* (Sir William Meyer Lectures 1940–41), University of Madras, 1943
[67] Ibid., p. 167

trends, as the former ones had done in the past. A few examples may suffice to depict that change.

M. V. Krishna Rao judges Kauṭilya's reflections on human history as surprisingly reasonable and astonishingly modern. He even goes so far as to call the ancient author a "state socialist", who created a "Social Welfare State".[68]

T. N. Ramaswamy praises as the most important part of *Artha-śāstra* that in which the state's economic planning policy is treated, and it is, he thinks, of immense value as an example for India's present policy.[69]

Even the well-known work of A.S. Altekar, *State and Government in Ancient India* (1st ed., 1949; 3rd ed., 1958), distinguished by its great critical scholarship and originality, cannot escape the present when dealing with the past. Altekar wrote:

> "Free India has embarked on the pattern of the mixed economy, as was the case with ancient India. We have however to see to it that the growing sphere of state socialism does not eliminate or cripple private industries and corporate enterprise. If the state runs the key industries and controls the rest, if it encourages the local bodies and city corporations also to enter the field of production and constructive nation-building activities, we shall have an economic structure, more or less similar to that in ancient India and likely to meet the needs of the time."[70]

The past economic system, as deduced from *Arthaśāstra*, was to form the model of the future!

Also Bhaskar Anand Saletore, though he rejects the idea of modern theories existing in the past, looks upon Kauṭilya as a "realist", to whom the concentration of power by the state was no more than a means to be used for creating a maximum of social welfare.[71]

The balanced system of power in the Mauryan Empire was the example recommended by B. G. Gokhale in his book *The Making of the Indian Nation* (1958). He admired the delegation of power to the different provinces, districts, and villages, combined with a maximum

[68] M. V. Krishna Rao, *Studies in Kauṭilya* (2nd ed., Delhi, 1958), pp. 44 f. and 202

[69] T. N. Ramaswamy, *Essentials of Indian Statecraft*. Kauṭilya's Arthaśāstra for Contemporary readers (London, 1962), pp. 24 f., 31 and 33

[70] A. S. Altekar, *State and Government in Ancient India* (3rd ed., Delhi, 1958), p. 384

[71] Bhaskar Anand Saletore, *Ancient Indian Political Thought and Institutions* (London, 1963), pp. 57, 531 and 580

of centralization of government. It was a noteworthy fact for him that "the Maurya state was highly bureaucratic and the hierarchy of officials working for it offers striking resemblance to governmental work in modern days".[72]

Krishna Chaitanya employed present-day political vocabulary in describing Kauṭilya's work in *A History of Sanskrit Literature* (London, 1962). He wrote, "Like Bismarck, Kauṭilya tried to steal the thunder from democratic socialism by showing that an absolute monarchy could also be a welfare state". On war and imperialism in *Arthaśāstra*, Chaitanya concluded:

> "A state of war – either 'cold' or 'hot' war – was the natural relation between states . . . He [Kauṭilya] was not interested in cultural subjugation. Though an implacable imperialist, Kauṭilya is at least free from the irritating cant of European imperialism in its colonial adventures. There is no talk about the secret mission of carrying culture to the benighted."[73]

K. M. Panikkar recognized not only a similarity of state and politics between Ancient and Modern India, but an uninterrupted continuity in the fields of revenue system, bureaucracy, and police. He sums up as follows: "If Indian administration today is analysed to its bases, the doctrines and practice of Chanakya [i.e. Kauṭilya] will be found to be still in force."[74]

In this summary, the Marxist-influenced historical writings on Ancient India should not be left unnoticed. S. A. Dange recast Jayaswal's *paura-janapada* theory in such a way that he saw in the ancient Parliament the representative assemblies of the property-owning classes. The development of the means of production was the main reason for the growth of property ownership and the antagonism between exploiter and exploited", "and gave birth to that affliction of human society, the State, the instrument of the exploiting class for violent suppression of the exploited class, in the name of 'saving society' ".[75]

Damodar Dharmanand Kosambi though a Marxist, did not agree

[72] B. G. Gokhale, *The Making of the Indian Nation* (Bombay, etc.), pp. 20 f.

[73] Krishna Chaitanya, *A New History of Sanskrit Literature* (London, 1962), pp. 124 ff.

[74] K. M. Panikkar, *A Survey of Indian History* (Bombay, etc., 1957; 1st ed., 1947), p. 29

[75] S. A. Dange, *India from Primitive Communism to Slavery*. A Marxist Study of Ancient Indian History in Outline (4th ed., New Delhi, 1961; 1st ed., 1949), p. 153

NATIONALIST INTERPRETATIONS 63

with this Marxist interpretation of ancient Indian history, and he vehemently contested Dange's interpretative excercises by stating that "Marxism is not a substitute for thinking, but a tool of analysis which must be used with a certain minimum of skill and understanding, upon the proper material".[76] In his very stimulating and thought-provoking book, *An Introduction to the Study of Indian History* (1956),[77] he devoted twenty-seven pages to a description of the Maurya state. He saw in Kauṭilya neither a pre-bourgeois Bismarck nor a Machiavelli, but a political thinker who stood in a long tradition of government which needed a few steps only to consolidate the Universal Empire.[78] Kosambi, who found in Ancient India hardly any trace of slave-trade, praised the relationship between the bourgeois upper class and the free, though not property-owning working class.[79] The policy of territorial expansion too found a positive evaluation: it served merely the aim of settling people on hitherto unsettled land.[80]

To summarize, the impact of *Arthaśāstra* on the modern Indian mind was twofold. It gave a strong "historical" basis and ideological impulse to Indian nationalism; furthermore, it promoted the "emancipation" of Indian historical writing from European, particularly British, concepts, which resulted in breaking the spell of the long-nourished European clichés about India.

The great interest of Indian historians in Ancient Indian politics since the discovery of *Arthaśāstra* is partly explicable as a reaction against the teaching of British "imperialist" historiography, which provided a historical justification for the maintenance of the British Raj. *Arthaśāstra* supplied Indian historians with a source that could be referred to in challenging English argumentation. It was proof of the existence of a highly sophisticated system of political thought in Ancient India besides the abundance of philosophical systems dealing with metaphysical problems, which till then had been looked upon by Europeans as the only sphere of Indian intellectual interests, and which had been the only source of pride of Indian historians and politicians. Now, history came to be interpreted in an Indian way, and it served the National Movement as an "ideological" weapon in the struggle for independence. Historical writing was the battlefield upon which the

[76] D. D. Kosambi, "Marxism and Ancient Indian Culture", in *Annals of the Bhandarkar Oriental Research Institute*, vol. 29 (Poona, 1949), p. 277
[77] Cp. Dietmar Rothermund, "Neue Dimensionen der Geschichte Indiens", in *Indo-Asia* (April 1964), p. 159
[78] D. D. Kosambi, *An Introduction to the Study of Indian History* (Bombay, 1956), p. 205
[79] Ibid., pp. 220 and 215   [80] Ibid., p. 218

ideological struggle between British Imperialism and Indian Nationalism was fought. The interconnection between politics and historical writing was an unavoidable consequence of a coincidence of impulses, affecting historical research through the discovery of *Arthaśāstra*, and the National Movement through the growth of radicalism at the partition of Bengal.

Without forcing the different phenomena into a Procrustean bed of uniformity, one can distinguish different periods of varied preoccupations in historical writings on *Arthaśāstra*. Till the mid-twenties the constitutional set-up of the ancient Indian state was of primary interest to historians. This preoccupation met the wish of the nationalists to prove India's capacity for self-government in the past and her maturity for it in the present. Till the end of the First World War the ancient Indian state was described after the model of the British Empire and the English constitutional system. In the years after, the relationship between imperial power and constitutional representation was investigated. Jayaswal's concept of a constitutional system of Ancient India with two houses of Parliament gained the widest popular support.

Towards the mid-twenties, the immediate interest in the constitution and the English models vanished. The economic and social system of the state in *Arthaśāstra* attracted the attention of historians. The German Reich of 1871 and Bismarck's social legislation were frequently referred to as modern embodiments of Kauṭilya's achievements. The growing impact of ideologies like socialism upon the Indian National Movement till Independence is also reflected in the writings on *Arthaśāstra*. The ancient Indian state provided an abundant field in which to search for examples of the future economic and social structure of India as visualized in modern ideologies. Since Independence, Kauṭilya's state has been frequently interpreted as an ancient type of a welfare state, based on a planned economy and liberal socialism.

The quest for actuality in past periods, particularly in ancient times, seems to be a general trend in modern Indian historical writings. Ancient India became the horn of plenty of modern ideas, present aims, and future hopes. This quest stands in marked contrast to the romantic backward orientation that can be observed in nineteenth-century Indian thought, which aimed at the revival of the "Golden Past" for a better future. The interpretations of *Arthaśāstra* reveal the opposite trend, namely to read future aims back into the past.

However strong the impact of nationalist aims upon the literature dealing with *Arthaśāstra*, there is no doubt that the new vistas of

Ancient India opened by the discovery of this political treatise had a tremendous impact on the concepts of Indian history at large. Many old clichés based on ignorance and prejudices proved to be groundless. *Arthaśāstra* was convincing proof that Indian history, meaning political history, was much too complex and subject to change to be adequately summed up in terms like "Oriental despotism", "social stagnation", "lack of a sense of history and politics", etc. It is hardly surprising that in this process of reinterpretation of Indian history the pendulum should have swung to the opposite extreme; and there is no denying that some of the interpretations overstepped the mark, mostly from a preoccupation with present-day national politics.[81] Yet, even Jayaswal's most provocative interpretation must be given the credit of having stimulated further research on the subject in India as well as in Europe.

The lasting contribution to Indian history made by the different interpretations of *Arthaśāstra* was the opening of the subject of Ancient India to historical research at large. Before, it had been the object of detailed research by specialists in inscriptions and philology, in numismatics and religio-philosophic literature, etc., who had been engaged on the sisyphean task of collecting, deciphering, and combining a huge amount of detailed facts. *Arthaśāstra* was a "living" monument of a man, or a group of men, standing in the midst of political life in Ancient India. It provided an inner connection and a lively background to the mass of detailed information previously collected.

Arthaśāstra provides an impressive picture of the political organization of the Maurya Empire. The edicts of Aśoka, the grandson of Chandragupta Maurya, came to be seen in a new light: not only their religious and spiritual message, but their political meaning, were revealed. In fact, Kauṭilya's and Aśoka's writings reveal an astonishing richness of political thought in Ancient India, which prohibits any black-and-white painting of this remote period. Indian thought was not as fundamentally different from that of contemporary Greece as had been maintained in nineteenth-century Europe. Kauṭilya, if he was Chandragupta Maurya's Minister, must have written his book on politics only a few decades after Plato had completed his *Republic* and a few years after Aristotle had finished his *Politics*.

The newly discovered political history of Ancient India gave Indian historians and politicians that "national" and "historical" confidence that was indispensable for a successful struggle for independence. It

[81] Cp. Julius Jolly, "About the old Political Literature of India and the Various Writers", in *Sir Asutosh Memorial Volume* (Patna, 1926–28), part ii, p. 137

E

provided the ammunition necessary to break the stronghold of the British Raj, which was fortified by the ideology of European, primarily British, but even Indian, historical writing. *Arthaśāstra* was for Indians a favourite armoury in the struggle for the intellectual and political independence of their country.

LORD CURZON AND
INDIAN NATIONALISM – 1898–1905

By S. Gopal

LORD CURZON HAD BEEN anxious, from the start of his public career, to be Viceroy of India. He was captivated by the allurements and the demands of the post, and he believed that he was destined to hold it. But Curzon was not inspired solely by personal ambition; he had also a sense of mission in India. He was convinced that it was the duty "laid on Englishmen from on high"[1] to maintain the Indian Empire, which was "the miracle of the world"[2] and "the biggest thing that the English are doing anywhere in the world".[3] Curzon was also honest enough to recognize that this Empire was of advantage to Britain. "As long as we rule India we are the greatest Power in the world. If we lose it, we shall drop straight away to a third-rate Power." [4] So duty and interest taken together made him

"an Imperialist heart and soul. Imperial expansion seems to me an inevitable necessity and carries a noble and majestic obligation. I do not see how any Englishman, contrasting India as it is with what it was or might have been, can fail to see that we came here in obedience to what I call the decree of Providence for the lasting benefit of millions of the human race. We often make great mistakes here; but I do firmly believe that there is no Government in the World that rests on so secure a moral basis, or is more fiercely animated by duty." [5]

Curzon was aware that "a sort of national feeling" was slowly growing up in India; and he added "I sometimes wonder whether a hundred years hence we shall still be ruling India". But he saw no

[1] Curzon to Sir Denzil Ibbetson, Member of the Viceroy's Council, 26 April 1904. Curzon papers, India Office Library, vol. 209, pt. ii, no. 122a

[2] Curzon to Sir Francis Younghusband, 19 September 1901. Curzon papers, vol. 182, pt. ii, no. 23

[3] Curzon to Balfour, 31 March 1901. Curzon papers, vol. 181, pt. ii, no. 211

[4] Ibid.

[5] Curzon to John Morley, 17 June 1900. Curzon papers, vol. 181, pt. ii, no. 119

reason why British rule should not continue indefinitely. He did not believe that the purpose of an alien administration was to prepare for its own withdrawal. India could be held by convincing the mass of the people that British rule was juster, purer and more beneficent than either any other foreign rule or the rule of Indians themselves. The Viceroy should act as a benevolent despot, going everywhere, seeing everything, and treating his subjects with sympathetic impartiality. The Government should secure the support of the loyal elements in the community, pursue the path of unwavering justice, redress grievances and anomalies wherever found, make British authority essential to the people by reason of its combined probity and vigour, insist upon a juster and more generous recognition of India by Britain and perpetually build bridges over the gulf that separated the Indians and the British.[6]

To Curzon, therefore, the task of the Indian viceroyalty was essentially one of administration. To use his own phrase, he energized the government all along the line; and he raised the standards in every department of public affairs. He had no high opinion of Indians.

"They are very strange people, these natives; they have such an extraordinary respect for strength of decision and action that, if it be based upon sincere purpose, and expressed in sympathetic language, there is scarcely anything that they will not accept from their rulers, however contrary to their own previous utterances or prepossessions."[7]

But he attached particular importance to the improvement of relations between the two races and the removal of the impression that the British Government were unjust or indifferent to India's interests. He shocked the officials of the India Office by sending a telegram of congratulations to the principal of a college at Poona on one of its students (R. P. Paranjpye, now Honorary Fellow of St John's College) securing the Senior Wranglership at Cambridge. He took the sternest view of cases in which Europeans were guilty of assaulting Indians. In 1899 and 1902, when the regimental and civil authorities sought to protect British soldiers accused of such crimes, Curzon had the regiments collectively punished and their commanding officers censured;

[6] Curzon to the Warden of Merton, 2 May, and to Morley, 17 June 1900. Curzon papers, vol. 181, pt. ii, nos. 92 and 119. Curzon to Balfour, 31 March 1901. Curzon papers, vol. 181, pt. ii, no. 211. Curzon to Salisbury, 21 June 1903. Curzon papers, vol. 162, pt. ii, no. 43

[7] Curzon to Lord George Hamilton, Secretary of State, 25 January 1900. Hamilton correspondence, India Office Library, D 510/4, Folio 73 ff.

and the civil authorities were publicly rebuked. Even the intervention on the second occasion of King Edward VII could not induce him to change his decision.

"If it be known that the Viceroy, backed by the Secretary of State, will stand up even against the crack regiment of the British Army, packed though it be with dukes' sons, earls' sons and so on – then a most salutary lesson will be taught to the army. If we yield to military and aristocratic clamour no viceroy will dare to go on with the work that I have begun." [8]

Throughout his seven years in India, Curzon also persistently urged the British Government and those who could influence British public opinion to show interest in, and regard for, the Indian people and not to practise an extortion "that would shame the combined ingenuity of the usurer and the attorney".[9] He desired that India should be lifted from the level of a dependency to the position which was bound one day to be hers, if it was not so already – that of the greatest partner in the British Empire. Never did Curzon hesitate to plead India's case as he saw it. "My first duty lies to my constituents and they are the people of India. I would sooner retire from my post than sacrifice their interests." [10] He began the tradition of the British Indian Government associating themselves wholeheartedly with the protests of Indian opinion against the policies of the South African Governments. "The name of South Africa", he wrote,[11] "stinks in the nostrils of India." During these years of Curzon's viceroyalty Gandhi was in South Africa and appreciated the Viceroy's efforts. He wrote of Curzon in May 1901 as "the strong and sympathetic Viceroy" and this letter was forwarded by the Government of India to Whitehall.[12] In 1902 Gandhi expressed a desire to wait in deputation on Curzon, but the Viceroy thought that if he received Gandhi it might be resented as undue pressure.[13] On 20 May 1905, long after Curzon had become

[8] Curzon to Hamilton, 27 November 1902. Hamilton correspondence, D 510/12, Folio 307 ff.

[9] Curzon to Lord Northbrook, 21 July 1902. Curzon papers, vol. 182, pt. ii, no. 103

[10] Curzon to Sir Arthur Godley, Permanent Under-Secretary, India Office, 17 December 1903. Curzon Papers, vol. 162, pt. ii, no. 94

[11] Curzon to St John Brodrick, Secretary of State, 15 November 1903. Curzon papers, vol. 162, pt. ii, no. 87

[12] *The Collected Works of Mahatma Gandhi*, vol. iii (Delhi, 1960), p. 189

[13] Curzon to M. C. Turner, 21 January 1902. Curzon papers, vol. 205, pt. ii, no. 13

unpopular in India, Gandhi wrote an editorial commending Curzon's "watchful guardianship" of the interests of Indians in South Africa.[14] With this general goodwill which he had built up, Curzon was confident that he could ignore the demands for political advance.

"The real difficulty in India, my dear Godley, is this. I am thirsting after administrative reform in every direction . . . my one object being to make our administration equitable, and our dominion permanent. The advanced natives care about little but constitutional reform. They want to get a larger share of the government of the country; and they count justice, equity, sympathy, the even hand, as of little account compared with a larger control of the executive, for which they are as yet profoundly unfitted and which they will never get from me." [15]

He disliked the Indian National Congress which had been founded in 1885 as the political organization of educated Indians, and regarded it as, if not actually disloyal, far from friendly to the Government. Romesh Dutt, a retired member of the Indian civil service, was president of the Congress in 1899. He had communicated to Curzon his appreciation of the great importance which seemed to be attached by the Viceroy to the conciliation of all sections of the Indian people; and in his presidential address he asked the Government to secure the co-operation of Indians. Sir William Wedderburn, another retired member of the Indian civil service, who was prominent in the councils of the Congress, suggested to the Viceroy that he establish a "national Government" by winning for British rule the sympathy of educated Indians.[16] Lord George Hamilton advised that as it was difficult to meet the aspirations of "young India" it was worth while encouraging "older India". [17] But Curzon saw no need to placate any Indians, young or old. He thought that India was filled with more loyal sentiments than at almost any previous time, and that the Congress was not the voice of India. From the start he treated that body as "an unclean thing" and was determined to reduce it to impotence by taking no notice of it.[18]

[14] Indian Opinion
[15] Curzon to Godley, 9 April 1901. Curzon papers, vol. 160, pt. ii, no. 27
[16] Dutt to Private Secretary to Viceroy, 15 September 1898, and Wedderburn to Curzon, 9 March 1900. Curzon papers, vol. 181, pt. i, nos. 51 and 98
[17] Hamilton to Curzon, 5 January 1900. Hamilton correspondence, C126/2, Folio 2 ff.
[18] Curzon to Wedderburn, 31 October 1900. Curzon papers, vol. 181, pt. ii,

The Congress, which had developed as a body of loyalist Indian opinion, was embarrassed by the unqualified hostility of Curzon and made a fresh approach. Dinshaw Wacha, president of the Congress in 1902, appealed to the Viceroy to consider the resolutions of the Congress with justice and sympathy, which, said Wacha,[19] were the two watchwords of Curzon's administration. To this letter there seems to have been no reply. Wedderburn wrote again, requesting Curzon for a friendly if informal recognition of the Congress as a responsible body expressing the Indian view on Indian affairs; and he was told that no co-operation was possible as the Congress tried both "to guide the counsels of the respectable reforming party and at the same time to keep in with the extreme men, who want something very different".[20] But Curzon was dishonest in suggesting that the Government would be willing to co-operate with the Congress if it remained a party solely of moderates. There was no Indian more distinguished for his moderation and rectitude than Gopal Krishna Gokhale, a member of the Viceroy's legislative council. Curzon, on the recommendation of the Bombay Government, gave Gokhale a title and wrote to congratulate him. Gokhale responded with enthusiasm:

"Your extremely generous terms will always be cherished by me with profound gratitude; and they will be a source of constant encouragement to me in the work to which my best energies have been and will always be humbly devoted – bringing the two races closer together in this land, so that the purpose of Providence in bringing India under British rule may best be realized by both." [21]

Yet Curzon never sought to utilize the services of Gokhale.

In 1903 Curzon believed that he had begun to lose the support of educated Indians. "No angel from Heaven could satisfy the Native party or escape being the victim of their incessant abuse." [22] In fact Indian opinion was still hopeful, despite such indications of Curzon's political temper as the Bengal Municipalities Bill, that the Viceroy

no. 160. Curzon to Ampthill, 15 June 1903. Ampthill papers, India Office Library, vol. 17
[19] Wacha to Private Secretary to Viceroy, 7 March 1902. Curzon papers, vol. 205, pt. i, no. 96
[20] Wedderburn to Curzon, 10 July 1902, and Curzon to Wedderburn, 15 August 1902. Curzon papers, vol. 182, pt. i, no. 121 and pt. ii, no. 116
[21] Gokhale to Curzon, 1 January 1904. Curzon papers, vol. 209, pt. i, no. 1
[22] Curzon to Salisbury, 21 June 1903. Curzon papers, vol. 162, pt. ii, no. 43

would not regard equitable administration as an end in itself. The nationalist leader Bepin Chandra Pal wrote that the Viceroy was the only man who had persistently sought to maintain British character in India.[23] Full disillusionment came only in 1904 when the Viceroy made clear that he had no regard for the views and sentiments of Indians and that they should accept whatever Curzon believed was good for them. This change in the Indian attitude to Curzon was expressed in revealing terms by Wacha.

"The person who said that Lord Curzon was an *Asiatic* viceroy will prove true. He has forgotten English methods of governing India and is daily growing in love with *Asiatic* ways of ruling. What a fall is here. This Viceroy will leave the country the most odious and hated, aye, worse than Lord Lytton." [24]

The next year Wacha congratulated Gokhale on laying low in the legislative council "the exalted python who has been so viciously doing mischief all round".[25]

The final loss of faith in Curzon had been effected by his decision to partition the province of Bengal. To the Viceroy it was essentially a measure of administrative reform. In April 1902 he had casually remarked that Bengal, with a population of 78.5 millions, was too large a charge for a single individual;[26] and when in the summer of 1903 he found that his officials were already at work on a scheme to divide Bengal, he gave it his general approval.[27] In December 1903 the proposals to transfer to Assam the three populous eastern districts of Bengal were published. There were certainly administrative advantages in this; but to public opinion in Bengal, partition appeared as an attempt to diminish the status of the province and to destroy the unity of the Bengalis. This was a correct assessment of official, if not of Viceregal, thinking. The Lieutenant-Governor of Bengal expected partition to weaken the influence of the eastern districts which were "a hotbed of the purely Bengali movement, unfriendly if not seditious in character". The Home Secretary to the Government of India wrote:

[23] Article in *Hindustan Review*, Allahabad, June 1903
[24] Wacha to Gokhale, 4 February 1904. Gokhale papers, National Archives of India. (Italics in original.)
[25] Wacha to Gokhale, 20 March 1905. Gokhale papers
[26] Curzon to Hamilton, 30 April 1902. Hamilton correspondence, D510/11, Folio 59 ff.
[27] Viceroy's minute, 1 June 1903. Government of India files, Home Dept. Public A. December 1903. Proceedings 149 to 160

"Bengal united is a power; Bengal divided will pull several different ways. That is what the Congress leaders feel; their apprehensions are perfectly correct and they form one of the great merits of the scheme." [28]

Meetings of protest were held throughout Bengal, but Curzon refused to pay heed. He declared that he could not find a single argument in the hundreds of articles and letters published and speeches made, and that, if the interests of sentiment and historical association were allowed to prevail, they would prevent all administrative reforms. In December 1904 he refused to receive a deputation of the Congress and interpreted the suggestion as a sign that the Congress was in a mood to accept defeat. The Government went ahead with their plans, and the details of the partition scheme were published in July 1905. The agitation, far from dying out as Curzon expected, grew in intensity. In addition to meetings and processions, a boycott of British manufactured goods was organized in Bengal. Even the British Chamber of Commerce lent its support to the agitation because of reports that Curzon's purpose in dividing the province was to weaken the Calcutta High Court.

The partition of Bengal was carried out in October 1905, on the eve of Curzon's departure from India, and two months after he had resigned as the result of a sharp controversy with the Commander-in-Chief, Kitchener, on an issue that is of no historical importance. Curzon's final comment on the agitation in Bengal was that it had only been saved from being formidable by being childish. [29] He failed to discern that Indian nationalism had now ceased to be purely intellectual and had attracted emotional support, that it had for the first time secured a grievance which agitated not politicians only but many men of thought and feeling, and that it had evolved revolutionary techniques other than terrorism. The agitation of 1904 and 1905 stung a new robustness into the politics of Bengal and India. It had been left to Curzon, who despised the Congress, condemned his predecessors for patting infant Indian nationalism on the back, and would have nothing to do even with moderates like Gokhale, to provide the occasion for the rise of a strong and virile opposition.

[28] Letter of the Lieutenant-Governor, 6 April 1904 and note of the Home Secretary 6 December 1904. Government of India files, Home Dept. Public A. February 1905. Proceedings 155 to 167

[29] Government of India files, Home Dept. Public A. September 1905. Proceeding 302

THE EFFECTS OF THE
RUSSIAN REVOLUTION ON INDIA,
1917–1920

By Zafar Imam

RUSSIA'S CONTACT with India dates back to the twelfth century. But before the British conquest of India, it was mainly confined to traders and stray travellers. It was the British rule in India which brought the shadow of Russia over the sub-continent. Because of the so-called Anglo-Russian rivalry in Central Asia and on the borders of India, traditionally, it was always a desirable British policy to create an unfavourable impression of Russia in India. Tsarist and autocratic Russia was contrasted with liberal and democratic England, and an unfavourable picture thus emerged in Indian minds. But at least, through this propaganda, the Indian middle classes were made aware of Russia.

Therefore it was not surprising that, having known Russia in this way for a long time, Indian public opinion was affected by what happened there in 1917 and after.[1] But by that time Indian opinion had two distinct forms of expression; the pro-Government and the nationalist. The pro-Government opinion, as expressed in the English-language press and various semi-official organizations, was naturally powerful and influential. The nationalist opinion, on the other hand, could be found in the nationalist-owned English and vernacular press and through various nationalist organizations. It was vocal and as a rule at variance with the pro-Government opinion and Government policy.

Early reaction in India

The news of the February Revolution was enthusiastically received in India. All sections of Indian opinion, both the nationalist and the

[1] "Minaev [the noted Russian Orientalist and traveller] as well as a number of English writers were inclined to the opinion that the English themselves have been responsible for stimulating [India's] interest in Russia." P. M. Kemp, *Bharat-Rus* (Delhi, 1958), p. 231

pro-Government, joined hands in welcoming the beginning of democracy in Russia. But their underlying motives were very different. The nationalist welcomed it for its possible effect – the reform and the liberalization of British rule in their country. The overthrow of the despotic Tsarist régime was cited as a grim warning to the autocratic British Government in India, and, as a first step to avoid such a catastrophe, the repeal of all coercive and repressive laws was suggested. The nationalists were also deluded with the hope of a new liberal administrative change in favour of the Indians, as a result of the collapse of autocratic régimes all over the world, beginning with the fall of the Tsarist régime and ending with the defeat of the Kaiser.[2]

The pro-Government section, on the other hand, welcomed it for its repercussions on the conduct of the war. It was believed that the beginning of popular government in Russia would provide a deathblow to the German influence in Tsarist Russia. It would strengthen Russia's military position, enabling her to make an effective contribution to the Allied war efforts.[3]

For a country like the India of 1917 the interval between the February and October Revolutions was too short to allow any idea to form of the real ideological struggle underlying them. In the first few months after the October Revolution, few could have gathered from conflicting and confusing newspaper reports, still further diluted by censors, what that Revolution really stood for.[4]

However, the enthusiasm shown on the previous occasion was discernible this time as well. The official report on the Indian constitutional reforms, published in 1918, said:

"The Revolution in Russia and its beginning was regarded in India as a triumph over despotism notwithstanding the fact that it has involved that unhappy country in anarchy and dismemberment; it has given an impetus to Indian political aspirations."[5]

That the collapse of Tsarist despotism was the greatest single factor to impress India could not be doubted.

[2] "Ayudhaya" (Hindi), Allahabad, U.P. Native Newspaper Reports, Lucknow, 24 March 1917, p. 180

[3] Advocate of India, Bombay, 17 March 1917

[4] Censorship of war news was vigorously enforced in India: particularly, publication in India of the news about the October Revolution was delayed by nearly five days (see Bombay Chronicle, Bombay, 14 November 1917). This is not surprising in view of the fact that such censorship of Russian news was also imposed on Britain by the decision of the War Cabinet

[5] Report on Indian Constitutional Reform (HMSO, Cmd. 9109, 1918), p. 14

While the city folk got the news of the Revolution through news-papers, the people in the villages heard of the events in far-off Russia from the soldiers returning from various fronts in Europe and the Middle East after the end of the war. This was true of many villages in northern India, particularly in the Punjab, whence the bulk of the Indian army was recruited, which took part in the war and also in military operations in Transcaspia and in Central Asia.[6]

But it was among the nationalists that an interest in the Russian Revolution began. Leading journals both in the English and Indian languages published articles and commentaries on the happenings in Russia, emphasizing the force of nationalism working behind them. As early as 24 December 1917, a leading nationalist daily of Bombay, *Bombay Chronicle*, wrote:

"Our ideas of Bolshevik are very vague . . . we recognize the fact that they could never have met with the present success had there not been something in their programme that was attractive and of promise to serve the present fear. The Bolshevik came with a definite scheme which took into consideration the necessities of the peasants and promised immediate confiscation of lands for the people."

The nationalist daily of Calcutta, *Bengalee*, thus emphasized the national character of the Revolution:

"The movement was comprehensively national and its success was only made possible by the splendid co-operation between the populace and soldiers. But that co-operation in its final and practical expression was itself the result of a unity of patriotic outlook and sentiment which . . . had begun to manifest itself for some time."[7]

[6] Drawing upon local Soviet press coverage of the accounts of the soldiers of the Indian army who were reported to have deserted to the Red Army during the military operations in Transcaspia and Central Asia, Soviet scholars have also expressed similar opinions. One Soviet scholar remarks: "The information about the October Revolution penetrated into India with great difficulty. It passed through the Indian soldiers on the fronts of imperialist war in the Near East, Africa, France, the Caspian and other places" (*Velikii Oktiabr̕ i narody Vostoka Sbornik*, Moscow, 1957, p. 26 8). Another Soviet Indologist, A. M. Dykov, in his article "*Osveshenie Oktiabr̕skoi Revoliutsii v Indiiskoi politicheskoi literature*", expressed similar opinions (see *Zarubezhnaia literatura ob Oktiabr̕skoi Revoliutsii*, Moscow, 1961, p. 252). For an Indian view, see Khwaja Ahamd Abbas, "India and October", *New Times*, Moscow, no. 75, 1957

[7] *Bengalee*, Calcutta, 19 April 1918

The Madras nationalist daily, *Hindu*, offered this analysis to its readers:

> "Bolshevism is a red terror . . . But what is Bolshevism in its inner meaning but the undefined, unexpressed, unconscious sub-conscience of the people desirous of revealing itself as a national entity . . . The murders, the unrest, the spoliation, the breaking-up of laws are the labour pangs and symptomatic of a nation's apotheosis." [8]

The influential nationalist journal, *Modern Review* of Calcutta, published with the active collaboration of Rabindranath Tagore, printed a series of articles from January 1918 onwards on various Soviet organizations. The journal commented:

> "It is refreshing to turn from the chorus of abuses and misrepresentation directed against the Russian Soviets by the capitalist press to the illuminating sketch of the framework of the Soviet state . . . we are at last given an insight into the mighty efforts of the revolutionary Russia to organize herself and work out her communistic ideals. . . In fact, [the Bolshevik] is striving to make Russia better and nobler than anything she has ever been." [9]

Still another interesting article came out in *Bombay Chronicle* under the title, "Lenin, The Man and His Aims". The article ridiculed the idea that Lenin was a German spy and discussed his programme. It concluded:

> "If Lenin is successful, the February revolution will sink into insignificance before the November revolution, for its success is nothing less than the end of the upper middle class and the final triumph of the common people." [10]

Effects on Government policy during the war

The Revolution in Russia precipitated a sudden change in Government policy, which was expressed in its attitude to the question of Indian reforms. The policy of the Government on Indian reforms had always been marked by cautious delay and hesitant action. All the war-time pronouncements from Britain recognized India's contribution to the war and in return promised generous reforms giving more

[8] *Hindu*, Madras, 19 March 1918
[9] *Modern Review*, Calcutta, 3 June 1919
[10] *Bombay Chronicle*, Bombay, 11 January 1918

share to Indians in the administration of the country. But they envisaged reforms only after the victory of the Empire in the war. During the later stages of the war the official attitude towards the proposed reforms became all the more rigid. The emphasis of Government policy was not on preparing the country for the reforms, but on discouraging the nationalists from expecting much from any change of policy in favour of Indians. As late as July 1917 the Viceroy condemned the proposal of reforms, embodied in the "Nineteen Memorandam" prepared by the nationalists, as "catastrophic changes". In England, powerful opposition to any reform was growing. Meanwhile India, on the eve of the Russian Revolution, was in complete subjugation, and had fallen into the grip of depression and frustration. The Nationalist Movement as a whole was waiting hopefully for the end of the war, and no agitational programme was envisaged.

Under the circumstances, the sudden announcement of the long-deferred reform in August 1917 was indeed revealing. In August 1917, the internal situation in India was in complete control of the Government, and it did not warrant a drastic change of policy. The hasty character of the announcement was shown by the fact that it caught the Indian administration unaware and the top civil servants were not sure how to implement it.[11] Besides, the Montagu–Chelmsford report on reforms was prepared a year after the announcement, the actual reforms were not enacted until the end of 1919, and they came into operation as late as 1920. One of the major considerations in this abrupt change of policy – from a firm and uncompromising stand to reconciliation – was not only internal but also external. The precarious balance of the war was of course decisive. It was felt that a definite announcement on the future of India, promising more administrative autonomy to the Indians, would increase the tempo of India's war efforts, and also revitalize her interest in the immediate victory of the Allies. But the deepening crisis on the Eastern front and the process of the disintegration of the Russian army made it urgent to keep the Indians quiet, divert their attention from external events, and channel it to the need for safety and security of the Indian Empire.

[11] Lord Curzon thus wrote to the Viceroy on his own contribution to the Montagu Declaration: "It was, I think, mainly due to me that you got from the Home Government the pronouncement, which you repeated in your Council – indeed the actual words are mine." (Letter quoted in Earl of Ronaldshay, *The Life of Lord Curzon*, vol. iii, London, 1928, p. 168.) It is almost certain that the announcement, known as the Montagu Declaration, was in fact prepared by Lord Curzon and Austen Chamberlain. The India Office was thus caught very much unawares as far as its preparation was concerned

Edwin Montagu, the Secretary of State for India, who rushed to India after the August Declaration, noted with satisfaction in his diary that "my work these six months has helped because it has kept India quiet".[12] The Montagu Declaration and Montagu's subsequent visit undoubtedly served their main purpose, and successfully diverted India's attention from the external events for the moment. Significantly, the Montagu Declaration was made within five months of the fall of the Tsarist régime and before the Russian withdrawal from the war.

But a sudden announcement of major concessions to the Indian national aspirations precipitated a long, acrimonious political controversy in India. Those who had consistently opposed even minor concessions to Indians were perturbed by the sudden change of policy, and found it convenient to attack the proposed reforms by citing the Russian example. It was argued that, like the Russian intelligentsia, the Indian intelligentsia would also fail to carry out their responsibilities of governing the country efficiently if such responsibilities were thrust upon them too soon without adequate experience and training.[13] Lord Sydenham, a former Governor of Bombay and the president of the influential Indo-British Association, declared: "Russia had given us a striking illustration of what happened when authority was destroyed and 80 per cent of the people were illiterate. The result in India would be more disastrous still." [14]

In India, the pro-Government daily, *Pioneer*, started the campaign against reform as early as November 1917:

> "Verily Russia at present is providing the world with an object lesson of the dangers attending the premature acquisition of representative institutions before a country is fitted for them. Home rule in Russia has virtually been synonymous with no rule ... The moral is obvious and should be taken to heart by all impatient politicians in this country. Self-government, if it is not to degenerate into the negation of all government as in Russia, is a plant of slow growth and any attempt to force it prematurely can only result in misrule, turmoil and anarchy." [15]

Even the semi-official daily, *Englishman*, indulged in dubbing the

[12] E. Montagu, *An Indian Diary* (London, 1930), p. 338
[13] Sir Valentine Chirol, "Reform in India: The Russian Example", *The Times*, 10 June 1918
[14] *The Morning Post*, London, 30 July 1918
[15] *Pioneer*, Lucknow, 19 November 1917

Home Rulers as Bolsheviks. In reply, the organ of the Home Rule League, *New India*, hit back vehemently: "No Englishman who compares our most honoured leaders to Russian pro-German Maximalists deserves freedom of speech in these days." [16]

But similar and consistent propaganda added a new and effective weapon to the armoury of those who were against the reforms. The widespread nature of this propaganda emanating from influential Anglo-Indian sources compelled the nationalists to take a defensive position. They argued that Home Rule would not bring about revolutionary chaos, but that in fact a delay in reform could lead to a revolution. Characteristic of the contemporary opinions on this controversy was the following from a nationalist daily:

> "It is not the Home rule that brought about troubles in Russia: It is the revolution which is the parent of this chaos. Had the erstwhile rulers of Russia had the wisdom to make a timely concession of Home rule, there would have been no revolution and no outbreak of lawlessness and disorder . . . Reforms indefinitely postponed are inadequate in their scope and comprehension, and prepare the ground for revolt." [17]

Another nationalist organ said:

> "The challenge [of comparing India with Russia] may be accepted and the analogy is particularly true because in the bulk of illiteracy and fervency of intelligentsia there are strong resemblances between India and Russia . . . India is at an indefinite advantage when it presses for initiation of Congress-League Scheme, inasmuch as we have British connections. Neither vested interests nor the tranquillity of progress can reasonably suffer." [18]

Such strong reactions against the attempts to introduce Russian events into the internal politics of the country, for the purpose of frustrating the nationalist aspirations, compelled some nationalists to moderation. The ageing nationalist leader, Sir Surendranath Banerjee, advised his countrymen:

> "Nor should we overlook the fact that a wave of Bolshevism is sweeping through the world and filling the minds of the conservative section of the world in all these countries, England included,

---

[16] *New India*, Madras, 2 November 1918
[17] *Bengalee*, Calcutta, 25 November 1917
[18] *Bombay Chronicle*, Bombay, 21 December 1917

with a sense of nervous alarm and a solicitude to strengthen arms of law ... If, by our extravagant proceedings, the impression is created in England and the House of Commons which is dominated by a conservative majority that India needs strong executive measures, the prospect of responsible government will have been seriously jeopardized. Let us act as sensible men who are trustees of the future!" [19]

The impact on the Nationalist Movement

It would be an over-simplification of the Indian situation to suggest that this new awakening in India was brought about only by the Allied war aims and by the speeches of the British and American leaders.[20] The Soviet pronouncement on the right of self-determination of all nations had also played its role, though a minor one, in projecting the concept of self-determination and also its practicability on the Indian scene. Soviet influence even proved more far-reaching and effective than is generally understood because of the sharp contrast in implementing the principle of self-determination in Allied and Soviet policy. The Indian public saw for itself that self-determination was proclaimed by the Allies but was not applied to India. On the contrary, they noted that the Soviet Government not only promised but also implemented it in the former Tsarist colonies as well.[21]

The president of the Calcutta session of the Indian National Congress, held in December 1917, the first to be held after the Revolution, contrasted the despotic nature of British rule in India with that of her "free and self-ruling neighbours across the northern frontier", and declared that "in future unless India wins self-government, she will enviously look at her self-governing neighbours and the contrast will intensify her interest".[22]

The appeal issued by the Soviet Government on 24 November / December 1917 renouncing secret treaties, annulling the partition of Turkey and Persia, and proclaiming the rights of all people and nations to self-determination was heard in India as well.[23] It had its repercussions too.[24] The 1918 annual Congress session was preoccupied with

[19] *Bengalee*, Calcutta, 5 December 1917
[20] The official report on the Indian Reforms (1918) has very much emphasized this point. See *Report on Indian Constitutional Reform*, op. cit., pp. 21–2
[21] See "Dyerism or Bolshevism", *Bombay Chronicle*, Bombay, 20 October 1920
[22] *Indian National Congress Report* (Delhi, 1917), p. 22
[23] *Bombay Chronicle*, Bombay, 22 November 1917
[24] An Indian historian later correctly summed up: "The Declaration of the

the question of self-determination and its application to India. The discussion that followed the main resolution on the subject showed a remarkable mixture of the traditional hold of British liberalism in the Indian intelligentsia and their faith in the Allied war aims, and of the new finesse introduced by Soviet Russia's declared policy. The Congress session was swayed by Lloyd George's war speeches and President Wilson's Fourteen Points, and they were approvingly quoted. But for all its carefully inculcated British liberalism, when it came to actual implementation of the principle of self-determination, it appeared to be inspired also by the Soviet example. Madan Mohan Malviya, the president of the session, while defining and explaining how self-determination would apply to India, said in his presidential address that a congress of the people would be called which "will determine and declare what in its opinion should be the measure of reform which should be introduced in the country. Let the British government give effect to the principle of self-determination in India by accepting the proposal so put forward by the representative of the people of India." [25] The question of the "representative of the people" was for the first time brought into the picture in the context of self-determination. Mrs. Besant, who moved the main resolution, thus ridiculed the Government's attitude to self-determination:

"We say this in answer to the Government of Great Britain declaring that it cannot govern without these powers [i.e. coercion and despotism] . . . But the Czar of Russia could only govern with coercion. Are you then no better ruler than the Czar of Russia!" [26]

The Congress session carried a unanimous resolution demanding self-determination for India.

By embodying successfully the principle of self-determination both in its internal and external policies, the Soviet Government projected it on the world scene. The Soviet Government was considered justified

---

right of the peoples of Russia was indeed an explosive statement and all the natives of Asia working for freedom heard it with a new hope." K. M. Panikkar, *Asia and Western Dominance* (London, 1953), p. 250. The official historian of the Indian National Congress, Sitaramayya, related, for instance, how Gandhi heard it and reacted by seeking a clarification from the Viceroy on the authenticity of the report (P. B. Sitaramayya, *History of the Indian National Congress*, Madras, 1935, p. 254). He was presumably staggered by the promises included in the announcement.

[25] *Indian National Congress Report, 1918 Session* (Delhi, 1919), p. 18
[26] Ibid.

in demanding that other Governments should do what they had already implemented in their own country. The question was asked, if one country could do this, why not others, and why not Britain herself? Even in India these doubts manifested themselves and such questions were asked. At a public meeting in December 1918 the following resolution was unanimously adopted:

"Self-determination is a birthright of every individual as well as of every nation . . . In [place of autocracy] has been instituted the governance of the people by the chosen representative of the people. Even the remnants of autocracy have vanished in this war. Self-determination will now be the general rule throughout the world."[27]

In this connection, the gradual transformation of the nationalist opinion on this question is to be noted. Until the end of the war, the controversy among the nationalists revolved round the question of how to achieve some form of responsible self-government, but later it touched upon the principle of self-determination and its application to India.[28] The Delhi Congress of 1918, demanding India's right to self-determination, asked the Government to take the first step towards its realization by "a declaration of the rights of the peoples of India giving in effect the immediate repeal of all laws, regulations and ordinances restricting the free discussion of political questions".[29] The Nationalist Movement led by the Congress thereafter adopted an active programme of agitation mainly against the repressive laws which prepared it for a further advance towards demanding complete freedom ten years later. In the Indian context, therefore, self-determination represented a more comprehensive idea than that of self-government, and a definite step forwards in quickening the pace of Indian political development.

Besides these developments in the political consciousness of Indian public opinion, the rise of new forces in the country had slowly begun to transform the Nationalist Movement itself into a mass movement

[27] *Madras Mail*, Madras, 5 December 1919
[28] It could well be said that self-government and self-determination in Indian nationalist thinking meant two different political ideas, the latter more comprehensive than the former. Self-government as presented by the Home Rule Movement envisaged some form of administrative reforms in favour of Indians within the Empire, while self-determination laid equal emphasis on the attainment of self-government and on the repeal of coercive laws (see *Sitaramayya*, op. cit., pp. 253–5)
[29] *Madras Mail*, Madras, 5 December 1919

with a definite programme of action and campaign against British rule in India. The main factors contributing to the new awakening were: the rapid transformation of the Indian National Congress into a dynamic organization; the renewed activity of a tiny but determined group of men working to win freedom by terrorist and conspiratorial means; and lastly a sudden shift in Government policy from reform and concessions to repression after the war ended.

The new force coming up on the Indian political scene was the beginning of an organized working-class movement. There are indeed some records to show that labour organizations in some form were in existence in Bombay in the late 1880s, but they were in no sense properly constituted labour organizations. There were strikes in the Bombay and Madras presidencies over wage rates. There was a big strike in Bombay in 1908 against Tilak's imprisonment. However, it was in April 1918 that the first organized industrial union was founded in Madras by M. Wadia. The new labour union successfully organized strikes in Madras textile mills within six months of its existence, and by the year 1919 its membership had risen to 20,000.[30] From Madras the movement spread to other industrial centres and some noteworthy unions formed in this period were the Indian Seamen's Union (1918), G.I.P. Railwaymen's Union (1919), Ahmedabad Textile Workers Union (1920), and others.[31] However, the All-India Trade Union Council (AITUC) was not formed until October 1920, and this marked the beginning of a properly organized working-class movement on an all-India basis.

But the growth of the political role of the working class after 1917–18 was indeed meteoric. The end of the year 1918 was marked by a great strike in the Bombay cotton mills, and by January 1919 125,000 workers coming from practically all the Bombay mills were out of work. In April 1919, the response to the strike call against the Rowlatt Bill was amazing. In all, during the first six months of 1920 there were strikes involving 1.5 million workers.[32]

In fact, the beginning of the year 1918 was the beginning of an organizational period of the working-class movement in India. Obviously, the horrible working conditions in factories, rising prices and falling wages, and the fantastic profits amassed by the employers were the main causes of the beginning of the working-class movement

[30] H. N. Mitra (Ed.), *The Indian Annual Register* (Calcutta, 1920), p. 324
[31] For a full account see N. M. Joshi, *Trade Union Movement in India* (Bombay, 1938), p. 8
[32] R. K. Das, *The Labour Movement in India* (New York, 1923), p. 36

in India. But it is significant, and not a mere coincidence, that the Indian working-class movement began immediately after the October Revolution. Also, it is noteworthy that a desire for solidarity with the October Revolution and sympathy for it manifested themselves among the Indian working class right from the very beginning. One of the main purposes of the programme of the All-India Trade Union Congress, adopted in its inaugural session in 1920, was to serve as a "link between Trade Unions in India and the Trade Unions and Labour Movements elsewhere".[33] In spite of the close association of some leaders of the movement with the British labour movement, Singarvalla Chettiar, a noted labour leader of Madras and an old Congressman, moved a resolution in the first AITUC session for sending delegates to the Communist International, but it was rejected.[34] A year later, in its second conference, the AITUC unanimously adopted resolutions which expressed sympathy for the Russian famine and gave a call to the working class all over the world to abolish wars by international action.[35]

The English-language nationalist newspapers and even the vernacular press had now recognized the importance of the working class in the country and understood the effect of the October Revolution on them. *Maryada*, a Hindi journal, observed:

"The birth of Bolshevism in Russia has in a way changed the situation. It has placed an idea before the world according to which all are equal and all powers have been seized from the rich financiers and bankers, etc. . . . now these powers have been vested in workers, peasants, etc. . . . Seeing all this, the eyes of workers of other countries have also been opened and they have started thinking of gaining happiness in their lands by effecting similar reforms . . ." [36]

The overall effect of the October Revolution on the Indian labour movement must thus not be underestimated. Notwithstanding the Fabian orientation of some leading labour leaders like Joseph Baptisaa, W. Wadia, Lajpat Rai and N. M. Joshi, more confused and paradoxical because of their advocacy of the spiritual task of Indian workers,[37] the beginning of consciousness among the Indian workers

[33] *Report of the First Session of the All-India Trade Union Congress (AITUC)* (Bombay, 1920), p. 33
[34] M. N. Roy, *Future of Indian Politics* (London, 1926), p. 104
[35] Elvyn Roy, "The Crisis in Indian Nationalism", *Labour Monthly*, London, vol. 2, no. 2 (1922), p. 155
[36] *Maryada* (Hindi), Benares, September 1919
[37] See *AITUC Report*, 1920 and also p. 94 of this article

F

of their own importance, and of working-class solidarity inside and outside the country, was all the more quickened under the impact of the October Revolution. One of the earliest studies of the Indian labour movement, in an analysis of the causes of its beginning, pointed out that "the last but not the least was the Revolution in Russia which awakened the hope for a new social order . . . With the social minds surcharged with war spirits, political agitation and revolutionary ideals, the labour class could no longer remain patient and tolerant under old social wrongs to new economic disabilities."[38] Years later, Indian leaders and intellectuals emphasized the role of the October Revolution in quickening the pace of the development of the Indian labour movement.[39]

While in the agitational field new forces were coming up, conspiratorial and underground movements in India and abroad had attracted attention from all quarters. Foremost among them were the emigré movements outside the country.

The Ghadar and Hijrat movements,[40] though not inspired by Russian example, were the first of any Indian political organizations to establish contact with the Soviet Government. Many of the emissaries of the Ghadar party from Berlin and of the Hijrat movement from Kabul later made contacts with the Soviet Government. This is a long and interesting story which cannot be related here.

The growth of the political consciousness of the Indian nationalists, the beginning of the working-class movement, the sporadic terroristic activity and the flirtation of the Ghadar and Mahajreen emissaries with Soviet Russia greatly discomforted the Indian Government, and their suspicion of the Indian Nationalist Movement was aroused further.

---

[38] R. K. Das, op. cit., p. 36–7

[39] See Jawaharlal Nehru, *The Discovery of India* (London, 1946), p. 312

[40] The Ghadar party was founded in 1913 in San Francisco and it operated from Berlin. Its proclaimed objective was to "overthrow imperialist Raj in India by an armed national revolution presumably with the help of foreign sepoys". The Hijrat movement has Islamic orientation, and on religious grounds it was mainly directed against British rule in India. Muslims from India migrated to Afghanistan and continued their anti-British activity from Kabul. From 1915 onwards, a Congress Committee was functioning in Kabul which proclaimed a "Provisional Government for the Federative States of India" with Raja Mahendra Pratab as president and Professor Barkatullah as prime minister. They approached the Tsar and later the Kerensky Government for help but were turned down. The Soviet Government sent them an invitation, and established contacts with them.

Politics in India after the war

Meanwhile, a significant shift in British policy in India had occurred. As soon as the war ended, the Government of India showed less inclination to fulfil all their promises of reforms and concessions, given during the war and confirmed in the Montagu Declaration of August 1917. The All-India Congress Committee, the Executive Committee of the Indian National Congress, noted:

"Since the signing of the armistice, the people, however, feel that there has been a notable change in the attitude of the European community, official and non-official, towards Indian aspirations generally and reforms in particular." [41]

After the war, the Government caused disappointment by appointing a special commission under Justice Rowlatt. The commission was to enquire into "the criminal conspiracies connected with the revolutionary movements", and to suggest new laws to deal with the situation. On the other hand, the report on the constitutional reforms published early in 1918 greatly dismayed all sections of Indian opinion, and subsequently most of them refused to co-operate with the reforms. Moreover, in contrast to the delay in enacting the reform bill, the recommendations of the Rowlatt commission were rushed through the Imperial Legislative Council. The bill was passed in March 1918 against the united opposition of all the Indian members of the Council. The bill armed the executive with far-reaching powers to arrest and detain persons without trial and formal charges.

As before, the Russian factor in this reversal of policy was important. Once the pressure of the war was removed, the British Government were concerned with consolidating themselves in India against the new challenge of Bolshevism. The increasing momentum of the Nationalist Movement and the rise of a hostile power on India's border made this all the more urgent and important. In September 1918, Lord Chelmsford, the Viceroy, declared in the Imperial Legislative Council:

". . . the Russian Revolution which took place shortly afterwards was seized upon as a pretext on which to base claims to sweeping changes. I think those who sang a paean of the Russian events have since repented. Russia indeed has hinted a moral which it would do us all good to take to heart." [42]

[41] *The Indian Annual Register*, 1920, op. cit., p. 18
[42] Lord Chelmsford's speech on 7 September 1918; *Times of India*, 9 September 1918

Later, in 1919, addressing the budget session of the Imperial Legislative Council, Lord Chelmsford again warned the country of the menace of Bolshevism to India. He also informed the Council of the establishment of a special staff to deal with the danger of Bolshevik agents and propaganda.[43] The Government of India issued an ordinance prohibiting the circulation of all rouble notes in the country.[44] The purpose of this ordinance, as officially described, was to suppress the circulation of all the roubles which were believed to be reaching India in connection with Bolshevik propaganda.[45]

It was obvious that in the opinion of the Government the situation had not much altered since the war. In place of the German military danger, the new and more formidable menace of Bolshevism now threatened India. The official report for the year 1919 declared:

"With the termination of hostilities, it might naturally be supposed that the menace on India's north-western frontier, of which mention was made in last year's report, would disappear. But, in point of fact, the very completeness of Germany's collapse hindered the restoration of these regions of Central Asia, which had been disturbed by the pioneers of intrigues and agents of disintegration . . . To the German arms there succeeded the more formidable menace of Bolshevik ideas." [46]

The British Government, no doubt for their own reasons, rightly considered the rise of Bolshevism on India's border a potential threat to their supremacy on the sub-continent. Partly in view of this new threat, their attitude towards Indian national aspirations hardened all the more, and only limited concessions to Indians were granted in the Montagu–Chelmsford reforms of 1919. But in their preoccupation with the danger of Bolshevism, the British Government misunderstood the growing tempo of the Nationalist Movement, assuming it to have been mainly engineered by Bolshevik agents.

In 1918–19, the Indian National Congress decided to launch a

[43] Government of India, *India in the Year 1919* (Government of India Press, Calcutta, 1920), p. 61

[44] According to *The Times* (7 April 1920), 2·5 million sterling pounds worth of Russian roubles were drawn in the Treasury within the time limit of six weeks. The authenticity of the report, however, is open to question, in view of the very low volume of trade between India and Russia in 1917 (100,000 tons of cargo worth a total value of 5 million pounds), *Times of India*, Bombay, 24 November 1917

[45] *India in the Year 1919*, op. cit., p. 168

[46] *The Times*, 20 March 1920

protest movement against the Rowlatt Bills. The movement spread like wildfire, and the whole country was in the grip of strikes and agitation, which finally led to the tragedy at Amritsar. These unexpected developments completely upset the officials, and they entertained a strong suspicion that the whole movement was being engineered by Bolshevik agents.[47] Earlier, in March 1919, *The Times* published a dispatch from its Helsingfors Correspondent on the Bolshevik plan of financing and arming the Bolshevik movement in India.[48] Close on the heels of this mysterious report in *The Times*, serious disturbances actually broke out in Punjab in April leading to the Amritsar tragedy. *The Times* proudly took the credit for unmasking the Bolshevik plans for India before their execution and pointedly asked "whether this organized work on communication has any connection with the Bolshevik plans to raise revolution in India".[49] Inside India the cue was taken up by the semi-official and pro-Government press. The Bombay daily, *Times of India*, while calling attention to the sinister sequence of events, suggested that an "external organization was fomenting these troubles through an Indian revolutionary party".[50] On the other hand, after a few months, *The Times* in a leading article analysed such reports and boldly concluded: "Our view has always been . . . that the tentacles of conspiracy extended far beyond India and that (as has since been fully proved) the secret leaders were in touch with Russian Bolshevik movement." [51]

As I have shown earlier, the October Revolution indirectly helped in transforming the Nationalist Movement into a more dynamic mass organization. But in no way was Russian influence reflected in the nationalist policy and programme of action. The accusation that the movement was organized and helped by the Bolsheviks was probably designed to discredit it to the outside world and to crush it at will. Therefore, the denials of nationalist leaders remained unheeded by the Government. But such statements as one by the President of the

---

[47] In its report, the Hunter Committee, which was appointed to enquire into the disturbances in Punjab, recorded: "It was stated before us by some officials that these disorders were in their view the result of an organized conspiracy throughout the country to turn out the British Government. One witness even suggested that it was connected with, if not financed by, the Russo-German Bolshevik organization." *Report of the Committee appointed by the Government of India to investigate disturbances in the Punjab* (Cmd 681, 1920), p. 93

[48] *The Times*, 20 March 1919

[49] Ibid.

[50] *Times of India*, Bombay, 17 April 1919

[51] *The Times*, 16 December 1919

Bombay Provincial Political Conference, that "the people's acts do not represent Bolshevism; they denote the deep disappointments and intemperate antagonism to government's stubbornness breaking into lawlessness",[52] were in fact correct appraisals of the situation. But the Government were not in a mood to enquire into the real nature of the growing discontent in the country. They sought to justify stringent measures against the Nationalist Movement on the grounds of the impending dangers of Bolshevism. Officially inspired propaganda tended to exaggerate the possibility of a Bolshevik attack on India to such an extent that the country was asked rather naïvely to postpone all agitations and rally round the Government in order to thwart the impending attack. "Let us at this time of danger", said the leader of the now pro-Government Home Rule League, "drop all criticism of government and stand firmly by the government against the revolution, which means bloodshed at home and invasion abroad." [53] The propaganda, however, failed to impress. The president of the Bombay Provincial Political Conference, which met early in 1919, argued thus:

"The conditions in India afford a fine field for Bolsheviks . . . therefore we should suspend agitation at once and assist the government against the march of the Bolshevist brigade. But is it marching? We cannot accept pontifical pronouncements without some evidence."[54]

Gandhi also lashed at the propaganda in his characteristic vein and remarked: "I have never believed in a Bolshevik menace and why should any Indian Government fear Russian, Bolshevik or any menace." [55]

It was at the height of this controversy that the Third Afghan War broke out in April 1919. The first and immediate reaction in India to the Afghan War vis-à-vis the Revolution in Russia contradicted the officials inspired propaganda of a Bolshevik invasion of India. The Indian nationalists saw for themselves that the trouble came from other than Russian sources and precisely because of Afghan demands for that complete independence and sovereignty to which they themselves aspired for India. Perhaps this was the reason that a genuine sympathy for the Afghans was widespread in the country.

[52] The Indian Annual Register, 1920, op. cit., p. 294
[53] India in 1919, op. cit., p. 23
[54] Indian Annual Register, 1920, op. cit., p. 294
[55] M. K. Gandhi, Young India, 1919–1922 (Madras, 1924), p. 717

But, in official quarters, the Afghan attack was thought to be a prelude to Bolshevik invasion. Efforts were made to identify the Afghan War with a Bolshevik conspiracy to capture India, but these efforts failed to make much headway.[56] In this connection, attention was drawn to the activities of the Indian Provisional Government in Kabul, who were already in contact with the Soviet Government with the object of driving out the British from India. However, India was not prepared to purchase national freedom from others. Gandhi voiced the opinion prevalent among the nationalists at that time when he said: "I would rather see India perish at the hands of Afghans than purchase freedom from Afghan invasion at the cost of her honour." [57]

Afterwards, M. N. Roy denied the allegations: "From first-hand knowledge of the Congress Committee [i.e. the Provisional Government in Kabul], as well as Soviet Russia, we can say that the Congress Committee never indulged in any intrigue to substitute British rule by Afghans or any other foreign rule." [58] But the episode of the Afghan War gave a great setback to the fear of Bolshevik invasion of India.

The Ideological impact on the nationalists

Reference to contemporary writings and speeches of the nationalists suggests that attempts were made to understand the nature of the October Revolution. We have noted the far-reaching influence it exercised on the course of Indian politics. But taking the October Revolution as a whole with Bolshevism as an ideological sanction behind it, one is struck by the marked ignorance about it among Indians, though this was mingled with sympathy.

[56] The official view of the Afghan War was that it was inspired by the Bolsheviks (see *Papers Regarding Hostilities with Afghanistan*, H.M.S.O., Cmd. 324, 1919). Some private accounts of the official missions in Central Asia also emphasized the point. To quote one from that of Captain L. V. S. Blacker of the Baily Mission to Tashkent, who alleged that "it was the Soviet who organized the Third Afghan War" (L. V. S. Blacker, *Secret Patrol in High Asia*, London, 1922, p. 186). The allegation, however, could not be substantiated, in view of the fact that contact between the Afghan and Soviet Governments was not established until the Afghan War was over. Diplomatic missions were established after the signing of Anglo-Afghan Treaty on August 8, 1919. (See L. Fischer, *The Soviets in World Affairs*, vol. 1, London, 1951, p. 285, and E. H. Carr, *The Bolshevik Revolution*, iii, London, 1953, p. 250.) For the Soviet view see L. B. Teplinskii, *Sovetsko-Afghanskie otnosheniia, 1919–1960* (Moscow, 1961), pp. 14–20

[57] Gandhi, op. cit., p. 763

[58] *The Masses of India*, Berlin and Zurich, January 1927

The bloodshed and turmoil in Russia during the Revolution were very unwelcome to Indian minds. They were thought to be a necessary corollary of a revolution, no matter where it occurred. Srinivas Shastri, a leading Congress member of Madras, in a public meeting declared that he was "one of those who had acclaimed the Russian Revolution as a symbol of deliverance and regeneration", but later he came to look upon it as a historical calamity, because "the prophets who had foretold ruin and disaster had also proved only too true". [59] But as early as December 1917 a leading nationalist daily like the *Bombay Chronicle* sought to meet India's traditional abhorrence to chaos and bloodshed:

"The transition of Government from a personal to a popular type was attended with measureless anguish in Great Britain and in France. The Civil War, the Commonwealth and the French Revolution leap up as it were to restrain those who really judge that Russia pays too dearly for her escape from the worst tradition of autocracy and orthodoxy." [60]

In 1919–21, Gandhi, at the threshold of his career, with his pronounced views on violence, had repeatedly declared his dislike for revolutionary methods and the chaos that follows from them. Writing in his weekly, *Young India*, he remarked:

"India does not want Bolshevism. The people are too peaceful to stand anarchy. They will bow to the knees to anyone who restores order. Let us recognize the Indian psychology. The average Mussalman of India is quite different from the average Mussalman of the other part of the world . . . The Hindus are proverbially almost contemptibly mild. The Parsis and Christians love peace more than strife. Indeed we have made religion subservient to peace." [61]

Here it is necessary to keep in mind that the Indian intelligentsia understood the Revolution in Russia in the context of a general historical phenomenon closely linked with the history of Europe. Their favourite theme seemed to be drawing a parallel with the landmarks of European history, particularly the French Revolution. But because of the fact that the Revolution broke out in the Asian regions of Tsarist Russia (which were much better known in India than any

[59] *Madras Mail*, Madras, 18 May 1919
[60] *Bombay Chronicle*, 17 December 1917
[61] M. K. Gandhi, op. cit., p. 279

other part of the Tsarist Empire), mainly on its own, locally, and the prevailing conditions in Tsarist Asia and non-Tsarist Asia were, generally speaking, identical, it naturally aroused sympathy and admiration in India. A diligent study of contemporary writings and speeches confirms the view that much of the sympathy towards the Revolution was due to the similarity between colonial rule in Tsarist Asia and British India. There is no point in deriving satisfaction from the idea that British colonial rule in India was much more liberal and had inherited a semblance of democracy from the mother country as compared to the ruthless and brutal nature of Tsarist rule in Central Asia. In essence, the character of both régimes was very much the same and based on a common foundation. In its direct economic exploitation, in adopting a policy of "divide and rule" (Central Asian Amirs and Khans were very much like the ruling princes in India), and in keeping the people chained to a conservative, despotic and repressive régime, Tsarist Asia and British India matched each other in 1917. Without stretching this analogy too far, it could very well be pointed out that colonialism from the viewpoint of subject nations was essentially a negative phenomenon. This was as true of British rule in India, at least in 1917, as it was of Tsarist rule in Central Asia and other non-Russian regions.

It is indeed interesting that the Revolution in Russia in itself was considered to be a European event. But when it affected relations between the master and subject nations, it became more an Asian event; hence an object of special interest. As we have noted earlier, Soviet declarations of November/December 1917 created a considerable effect in India and other parts of Asia. In India this was acknowledged many years later by the leading intellectuals of Bengal in a statement which said: "We, in India, cannot forget how in one great gesture after the revolution the Soviets renounced all priorities and capitulations and concessions and other privileges of the former Tsarist Government in Asiatic countries." [62]

A century of careful inculcation of liberalism through education and other social reforms of a limited nature had created an atmosphere not conducive to revolution and its ideals. Hence the Indian intelligentsia vaguely admired the October Revolution, and looked upon it with a well-marked critical appreciation, while the restrictions imposed by the censorship made it all the more confusing and baffling. Therefore, the ignorance that prevailed about the October Revolution

[62] *New India* (India League, London), September–November 1941

was understandable and the confusion of the intellectuals was explicable. It was believed, for example, that revolution could come only through revolutionary propaganda of a destructive nature and that the objective conditions in a given country played little or no part in its failure or success. Characteristic of such opinions were the remarks of a leading Congress leader from Madras who said that "the revolution in Russia was brought about only by the great spread of ideas through decades of literature of a very revolutionary character".[63]

In this connection, the attitude of some leaders of the new labour movement was revealing. Labour leaders like Joseph Baptisaa and W. Wadia, though they recognized the evils of capitalism and the efficacy of the power of organized workers, boycott, strikes, and so on, preferred to assign a spiritual task to the Indian labour movement.[64] As chairman of the reception committee of the inaugural session of the AITUC, held early in 1920, Baptisaa invoked the "power and principle of organized labour" to throw "some light from the East to illuminate the darkness of the West . . . for the humiliating spiritualism of the East to chasten the brutalizing materialism of the West".[65] On the other hand, the president of the session and the Congress leader, Lala Lajpat Rai, even went so far as to say that "foreign capitalism must be opposed in common by all workers because the interest of workers all over the world is one and the same . . . The cause of the European proletariat is neither safe nor secure so long as there is cheap labour in China and India." [66] But, at the same time, he was opposed to Marxism because it would bring to India, the land of "mighty spiritualism, the evils of expiring industrial civilization".[67] Such statements were characteristic of these leaders, but it is doubtful whether they themselves realized the contadiction involved in their thinking. Yet it was a clear indication that they were now beset with doubts and confusion about all the values they had so far accepted without much questioning.

A very interesting book, by an author who was later to become a founding member of the Indian Communist Party, was written early in 1919 and published in 1921. Its interest lies in the fact that it clearly shows this ideological confusion even among the early socialists in India. The author, while comparing Gandhism and Leninism, tipped

---

[63] *Madras Mail*, Madras, 18 May 1919
[64] See *AITUC Report*, op. cit., 1920, pp. 17–18
[65] Ibid.   [66] Ibid., p. 19
[67] Lajpat Rai, *Political Future of India* (New York, 1921), p. 201

the scales in favour of Gandhism; yet he hailed the October Revolution as the beginning of a new era.[68]

Although the character of the Revolution was misunderstood, it left its mark on Indian literature. Munshi Prem Chand was a leading literary figure in the Hindi–Urdu languages. Before the Revolution in Russia, he had already emerged as a great patriotic writer of repute. Within a year of the Revolution, he wrote his famous article *Mahajani Sabhyata* (Bourgeois Civilization) in which he made a scathing criticism of the civilization of the exploiters, and vigorously defended the "new humanist culture" of Soviet Russia.[69] In one of his personal letters to a friend, he went so far as to declare that "I am now almost convinced of Bolshevik principle".[70] The date of this letter, according to his son, was between the years 1918 and 1919.[71]

Another notable and a romantic figure was the Muslim divine, Obaidullah Sindhi. He was one of the founders of many anti-British movements and a guiding spirit of the "Hijrat Movement". Obaidullah Sindhi, driven out of India, wandered through Soviet Russia and met some of the Soviet leaders. In Soviet Russia he saw a principal ally for the cause of India's freedom and wished the régime well.[72]

Quazi Nazrul Islam, the noted Bengali poet and writer, was the first Indian to write about the far-off events across the border. Early in 1918, Nazrul was serving as a private in the Bengali Regiment stationed in Karachi, where he wrote his story, *Byathar Dan* (The Gift of Agony), published in a contemporary Bengali language journal in 1919. The story showed how the writer, when in the army, heard stories about the Revolution in Russia and how deeply he felt for it. One of the main characters in the story was thus made to relate his adventure across the border: "Wandering a while, I have joined this Red Army. They [i.e. the Red Army] are convinced that this high and noble ideal of theirs is gaining ground in the hearts of men

---

[68] See S. A. Dange, *Gandhi vs. Lenin* (Bombay, 1921), pp. 24–6
[69] Ram Bilas Sharma, "Prem Chand and the Socialist tradition in Hindi literature", *New Age Monthly*, New Delhi, vol. iii, no. ii, 1959
[70] Ibid.
[71] Ibid.
[72] See Obaidullah's writings in Urdu, particularly his memoirs, though not yet complete, in Urdu Journal *Sirat* (Benares, 6, 1958). The Soviet journal *Zhizn' Natsional'nostei* published a long interview with him when he first came to Moscow in October 1919. In the interview Obaidullah Sindhi explained, at some length, his theological outlook, but praised Soviet Russia for championing the cause of Muslims and sought help for driving the British out of India. ("Indiiskii revolutsioner v Rossii", *Zhizn' Natsional'nostei* no. 40 (48), 1919, p. 2.)

all over the world . . . I, too, am one of that great organization." [73]
It is noteworthy how Nazrul got this idea of joining the Red Army
and that too for a noble and ideal cause.[74]

Concluding remarks

It is indeed true to say that during 1917–1920 the Indian Nationalist
Movement remained largely unaffected in its policies and programmes
by the October Revolution. The most marked effect of the October
Revolution was the quickening of the pace of the Nationalist Movement. It was also felt in the emergence of new forces, mainly the
Indian working-class movement; and, to some extent, in the conspiratorial and anti-British activities carried out by Indians outside the
country. In spite of their ignorance of the exact nature and character
of Bolshevism as such, there was also a marked sympathy for the
ideals and programme of the October Revolution among politically
conscious Indians, mainly through their belief that Soviet Russia was
opposed to British policy everywhere, and that her policies presented
something new and conducive to their own interest.

It is, however, paradoxical that while the October Revolution was
so well received in India and affected the political life of the country,
yet, at that time, the Revolution and socialism appeared to the Indian
leaders as something foreign to their country. In the midst of the growing upsurge of nationalism of that period, all things foreign were fast
becoming things least wanted and desired. The October Revolution,
however much appreciated, could not therefore have easily and
instantly moved Indians to follow its example. In essence, the character
of the Indian Nationalist Movement itself in 1917–1920, and the
nature of its leadership, was marked by a natural reluctance to go
further than was necessary and expedient. It was, therefore, not

[73] Muzaffar Ahmad, *Kazi Nazrul Prasenge, Smritkatha* (Bengali) (Calcutta,
1959), p. 59
[74] Two Indians, M. N. Roy and Shaukat Usmani, who were then active
participants in the Russian events, have referred to the desertion of Indian Army
sepoys to the Red Army in Turkestan and Transcaspia (See M. N. Roy,
"Memoirs", *Amrita Bazar Patrika*, Calcutta, 8 June 1952, and Shaukat Usmani,
Peshawar to Moscow, Benares, 1927, pp. 47–9.) One Soviet writer has quoted a
newspaper of Tiflis, *Volna*, to show that the Indian sepoys refused to obey the
commands of their officers in Gori (Georgia), and deserted to the Red Army.
(T. F. Deviatkina, "Vliianie Oktiabr'skoi revoliutsi na natsional'no-osvoboditel'-
noe dvizhenie v Indii (1918–1922)" in *Velikii . . . Sbornik*, op. cit., p. 269. See
also *In Common They Fought* (edited), Moscow, 1957, p. 75.) But such cases of
desertion could not be confirmed from the British sources

surprising that some of its leaders had to be extremely cautious, to save the movement from the charge of collusion with Soviet Russia – a charge which was then being levelled by the Government supporters and over-zealous Empire loyalists. Besides, the October Revolution in itself, partly because of the limitations and privations imposed on it by the Civil War and Intervention, was not able to reveal its full social and economic effects to India. The Indian Nationalist Movement realized its full significance only when the Indian movement acquired a real mass political consciousness, and developed a full awareness of the international aspect of India's fight for freedom. Later, from 1927 onwards, many Indian leaders and public figures visited Soviet Russia and came back with an admiration of her achievements. Marxism and socialism became the panacea of the rising new forces which greatly affected the political and social programme of the entire Nationalist Movement. These, however, made their mark in the 1930s and, as such, they are beyond the scope of the present article.

However, to all intents and purposes the October Revolution, for the first time, introduced an explosive new factor in Indian politics. This affected the policies of the British Government both internally and externally. Internally, it created a deep-rooted suspicion of the bona-fides of the Nationalist Movement partly because of the apparent community of interest between the Indian nationalists and Soviet Russia – which was largely accidental rather than designed, as far as the Indian nationalists were concerned. The British Government looked with alarm and suspicion at every demand the nationalists advanced and every agitation they undertook. In them the British detected a mysterious Bolshevik connection and failed to evaluate the nature of the growing upsurge of Nationalism objectively. In the external field, as a result of the October Revolution, an openly hostile power had arisen on the borders of British India. This suddenly posed the serious problem of defending the British Raj against any possible Soviet military aggression, and also of safeguarding it against a hostile propaganda campaign. The British Government became increasingly concerned with the safety and security of India, and their external policy had to be reoriented to meet this new challenge to their supremacy in India. In point of fact, as a result of the October Revolution, India thus suddenly became a major international issue and one of the main causes of friction between Soviet Russia and Britain.

NEHRU AND EARLY INDIAN
SOCIALISM

By Dietmar Rothermund

THE CONNECTION OF Jawaharlal Nehru with the socialist movement in India cannot be described in institutional or ideological terms,
because Nehru's political loyalties and doctrines were always highly
personal. He was the enthusiastic agitator and the detached mentor
who influenced a generation of Indian patriots and gave their thought a
socialist tinge. This process may be analysed by looking at three
aspects of Nehru's socialism. The first aspect is the element of Vedanta
philosophy in Indian socialism, the message of Vivekananda, which
influenced Nehru in his interpretation of the Brahminical ideal of
service and in his skilful use of socialism as an instrument of diagnosis
and therapy. The second aspect is Nehru's role as a radical mediator
who conjures up a new vision of the political development in the
important decade of 1927–37. The third aspect is seen in the evolution
of the economic programme of the Indian National Congress in
those years of the intensive political agitation for national freedom.

I

With Nehru, socialism was more of a sentiment and an attitude
than a system. His emotional commitment was stronger than his
intellectual convictions. But this also implied a constant quest for an
Indian expression of socialist thought. Marxist *mantras* would not
suffice. For Socialism to be meaningful to India it ought to be related
to some fundamental ideals of Indian life. This relation Nehru found
in the Brahminical tradition of service, in the spurning of the profit
motive as a value which ranked very low in the scale of India's social

Note on Interviews

Several interviews with Indian political leaders have greatly helped the author
in reconstructing this image of Nehru and Early Indian Socialism; first of all two
interviews with Nehru in 1962, and furthermore discussions with E. M. S.
Namboodiripad, Jayaprakash Narayan, Achyut Patwardhan, M. R. Masani,
Y. B. Chavan, and many others.

values. The Brahminization of Indian culture was most eloquently advocated by Swami Vivekananda,[1] who influenced Nehru in this respect. Nehru was aware of this influence and considered it to be one of the most important elements of his thought.[2] Like Gokhale, who once admitted that Vivekananda had voiced his own feelings,[3] Nehru was inspired by Vivekananda's vision of India's unity, by his emphasis on *karmayoga* as a means of redeeming the poverty-stricken people of India, and by his self-assured approach to the West. In a passage of his autobiography which in many ways reads like similar passages of Vivekananda's discourses, Nehru portrayed this attitude succinctly:

"Right through history the old Indian ideal did not glorify political and military triumph, and it looked down upon money and the professional money-making class. Honour and wealth did not go together, and honour was meant to go, at least in theory, to the men who served the community with little in the shape of financial reward.

"The old culture managed to live through many a fierce storm and tempest, but though it kept its outer form it lost its real content. Today it is fighting silently and desperately against a new and powerful opponent – the *bania* civilization of the capitalist West. It will succumb to this newcomer, for the West brings science, and science brings food for the hungry millions. But the West also brings an antidote to the evils of this cut-throat civilization – the principles of socialism, of co-operation, and service to the community for the common good. This is not so unlike the old Brahman ideal of service, but it means the brahmanization (not in the religious sense, of course) of all classes and groups and the abolition of class distinctions. It may be that when India puts on her new garment, as she must, for the old is torn and tattered, she will have it cut in this fashion, so as to make it conform both to present conditions and her old thought. The ideas she adopts must become racy to her soil." [4]

[1] Swami Vivekananda, *Selections from Swami Vivekananda* (Almora, 1946), pp. 206 ff. and 427

[2] Nehru emphasized his indebtedness to Vivekananda in an interview with the author on 31 January 1962

[3] *The Servant of India*, 20 February 1930, reference to a letter written by Gokhale to K. Natarajan in 1902

[4] J. Nehru, *Autobiography* (London, 1958), pp. 431–2

In this way socialism emerges as a means of cultural regeneration and the purity of the Brahminical ideal will be revived in the classless society. The Vedantic concept of self-realization, which was used by an earlier generation of militant nationalists in order to equate the quest for *moksha*[5] with national liberation, now suffused the new message of socialism so as to add a peculiarly Indian flavour to it. The dilemma of Marxist revolutionary doctrine, the definition and realization of class-consciousness, which led many of Marx's ideological heirs to a re-Hegelianization of their master's system, was obviated by the Vedantic element in Indian socialism, since the system of Vedanta was attuned to all subtle problems of consciousness.

In the Vedantic system, the diagnosis of the spiritual disease is at the same time its therapy. *Jnanayoga*, the contemplative method of self-realization, makes knowledge itself the means and the end of salvation. It is in keeping with this tradition that Nehru used socialism mainly as a means of analysis, hoping that this analysis itself would clear the fog of false consciousness and thus contribute to social and political progress. Many of his speeches sounded like verbal radicalism in the face of forces which he was neither able nor willing to subvert, and in many instances he actually developed a great skill of concealing a practical compromise behind a barrage of radical statements, which had the ring of sincerity. However, while a clever operator could hardly have maintained the ring of sincerity on such occasions, Nehru's faith in the ultimate truth of his assertions enabled him to reconcile the sincerity of his words with the art of the possible in his political actions. Socialist analysis also helped him to have a detached view of political decisions and to identify and classify the forces which he saw ranged against India's emancipation. By emphasizing the world-wide aspect of these forces he could always transcend the level of petty tactics of the National Movement and refer to the grand strategic alignments and to the inevitable progress toward a socialist future.

His analysis of the international situation reinforced his striving for national unity. He did not think that the socialists could achieve any progress in isolation from the national movement, and he stressed in most speeches that socialism could be achieved only after national independence. This was an additional reason for restricting socialism during the freedom struggle to the field of diagnosis and postponing the therapy. But seen from the point of view of the identity of diagnosis and therapy, this was only a postponement of the final consummation.

[5] *Moksha* = Salvation: for its equation with national liberation see for instance Bipin Chandra Pal, *The New Spirit* (Calcutta, 1907), p. 248

The socialist, due to his better insight, was bound to be the spearhead of the national movement. Therefore both the cause of socialism and of national liberation was best served by those who would strive for the one by working for the other.[6]

The identity of the socialist diagnosis with the quest for national unity was most obvious in Nehru's approach to the problem of communalism. To him Hindu and Moslem communalism were products of middle-class infighting utterly divorced from the consciousness of the Hindu and Moslem masses.[7] In this case diagnosis and therapy seemed to be most closely connected. If everybody would realize that economic interests were the one and only reason for communal jealousies, communalism would be deprived of its religious garb and thus appear as a non-entity, the *maya* of false consciousness, and national unity would be restored. This was also the line of reasoning which led him in later years to the equation: anti-communal = secular = egalitarian. An egalitarian society would serve as a stable foundation for a secular state and only the secular, national state could transcend the claims of communalism and prepare the ground for an egalitarian society.[8]

However, there are some inherent contradictions in Nehru's vision of national unity. He has not based his definition of this unity on purely economic terms, and he often referred to cultural values which are capable of arousing communal feelings even if treated in a secularized manner (his reference to "Brahmanization", which we have quoted earlier, is a case in point). Thus even his way of connecting socialism with the Hindu-tradition may not appeal to Moslem socialists, who would rather relate socialism to the corporate ideal of the *millat*, which is altogether alien to Hindu thought.[9] Nehru's socialist diagnosis of the communal problem was therefore bound to be challenged and he blurred his own vision by oversimplifying the issue.

The relationship of the middle class to the masses, which was so crucial to Nehru's analysis of communalism, preoccupied his mind in many respects, because it also affected his own role in national politics. Orthodox Marxist doctrine with its dialectical polarization does not provide a definite place for the middle class in its system. At the most

[6] Congress Presidential Address 1929, in *Congress Presidential Addresses 1911 - 34* (Madras, 1934), p. 884. See also J. Nehru, *Eighteen Months in India* (Allahabad, 1938), pp. 9 ff.

[7] Nehru, *Autobiography*, p. 140

[8] J. Nehru, *Letters to Provincial Congress Committee Presidents* (New Delhi, 1954), p. 20

[9] W. Cantwell Smith, *Modern Islam in India*, Lahore, 1943

G

this class is a transitory phenomenon which fades out of the picture with the intensification of the class struggle. The middling will have to join the one or the other. Nehru made very skilful use of this model, when analysing the psychology of the vacillating Indian bourgeois, who participates in the National Freedom Movement, but cannot be relied upon for any length of time. But he also admitted that the national leadership and even the leadership of the peasants' and labourers' organization had so far emerged only from this middle class, and that many of these leaders had proved to be of remarkable integrity, willing to sacrifice their interests and their lives.[10]

In the final resort he was unable to solve this problem theoretically and he restricted himself to a personal equation: a man who loved the Indian people and who was abundantly loved by them.

II

Nehru was in many respects the ideal type of the radical mediator, a kind of politician whom we encounter in many transitional societies, slightly alienated and detached but deeply in love with his country, a man who wants to transcend the limitations of his political environment both in terms of a new political vision and in a quest for untapped sources of power, and who must achieve in his own personality the emotional synthesis of the prevailing forces and the impact of modern trends.

Nehru was very well suited for this role. Even the date and place of his birth were very advantageous for his later career. He belonged to a province which emerged into the political limelight at the very moment when he started his political career; twenty years younger than Gandhi, he was the bright young man of the older leaders and the senior of the generation of young radicals who were born in the first years of this century.

Nehru's home province, the vast United Provinces of Agra and Oudh, a sprawling, disunited state, was an ideal breeding ground for agitational politics. Nehru as a Kashmir Brahmin belonged to a small minority which was intimately related to the vanished court culture of the Muslim rulers of this region, a minority which was socially respected but culturally marginal and was therefore doubly inclined to adapt to the Western impact, while maintaining a detached but profitable relationship with its environment. There was a dearth of

[10] *Congress Presidential Address* 1936, in J. Nehru, *India and the World*, London, 1936

leadership in this province, and in the early years of national politics the marginal minority of the Kashmir Brahmins dominated the scene. Respectable marginal minorities are usually rather moderate in their politics, and among the Kashmir Brahmins it was only the Nehru family that plunged into the more radical movement of the Gandhian era and thereby acquired almost a monopoly of radical leadership in this province. There were hardly any organizations which one had to capture in order to attain leadership in this province, but there was a vast store of inarticulate peasant populism which provided the small group of radical leaders with an enormous backdrop of potential unrest – an inexhaustible fund of goodwill, or should one say ill-will, which could be drawn upon so as to endorse any political programme. This vague populism accommodated a spectrum of leadership which would include the militancy of a radical Hindu like Purushottamdas Tandon as well as the secular socialsm of Nehru.[11] A pronounced conflict between indigenous capitalists who financed the national movement, and radical politicians, could not arise in the United Provinces, since the radicals directed their attacks against the badly organized landlords; in fact, the combination of a city-financed National Freedom Movement with agrarian populism was an ideal solution for the nationalist businessmen as well as for the radical politicians, even though there were occasional doubts on both sides as to how long this partnership would last.

For Nehru this provincial background meant an easy acceptance of radical views and an assured access to national leadership. When he left India for Europe in 1926 he was already an All-India figure and a seasoned politician who would look at the West in a different manner from the student who had left London in 1912.

A stay of almost two years in Europe gave Nehru a good deal of time to absorb new ideas and to place his political experiences in India in a world context. He participated in the Congress of the Oppressed Nations in Brussels and helped to start the League against Imperialism; he also visited Moscow and was impressed by the achievements of the Soviet Union. The formative experience of U.P. radical leadership with its vague populism was now surcharged with the exhilarating air of socialist internationalism. Again, in spite of all the intellectual overtones, this was first of all an emotional stimulus for Nehru. In his report to the Indian National Congress, as whose delegate he attended the Brussels conference, there is very little of ideological comment, but

[11] Nehru, *Autobiography*, pp. 298 and 310

many references which show how new vistas opened up before Nehru's eyes: the problems of the Latin Americans about which he had not known much before attending this conference, the Sanskrit names of the Indonesians – a striking symbol of India's cultural influence beyond the seas – the revolutionary fervour of the young Chinese delegates, the problem of Indian troops being used against the Chinese by the British, and the solidarity of British labour movements with the Chinese national movement.[12]

It is more by way of empathy than by means of ideological considerations that Nehru perceives a world on the march to socialism in those years of the European interlude. And it is this socialist empathy which enables him to communicate this feeling to the younger generation in India. Thus it comes naturally to him to avoid ideological jargon and to convey the message of socialism in terms of a personal appeal.

Popular radicalism, refined by the ennobling touch of internationalism, made Nehru an ideal national leader, but in the years after his return from Europe his socialist conscience was often in conflict with his claim to leadership. He was in office but not in power, as Gandhi put it,[13] and often he had to swallow his pride and endorse political decisions of which he disapproved. He believed that national unity and freedom could be achieved only if the unity of the National Movement was preserved and therefore he chose to abide by the party discipline. The older Congress leaders permitted him to preach socialism as his personal creed but prevented him from committing the Congress to a radical programme. This he accepted freely and whenever he spoke he openly stated these restrictions.[14] But it was frustrating for him that he frequently had to support in his official capacity certain measures and pacts which he had condemned previously. He had to break with the League against Imperialism when they attacked his stand on the issue of Dominion Status.[15] He was unable to get the Congress constitution revised so as to admit radical representatives of trade unions and peasant organizations to the ranks of the All-India Congress Committee.[16] He was often forced to resort

[12] For Nehru's report to the Indian National Congress about the Brussels conference and the League Against Imperialism see *Indian Annual Register* (Calcutta, 1927), vol. ii, pp. 152–9

[13] J. Nehru, *A Bunch of Old Letters* (Bombay, 1958), p. 197

[14] J. Nehru, "To My Friends and Critics", in *Eighteen Months in India*, pp. 9 ff.

[15] See B. R. Nanda, *The Nehrus – Motilal and Jawaharlal* (London, 1962), p. 257

[16] J. Nehru, "The Congress and Labour and Peasant Organizations", in Nehru, *Eighteen Months in India*, p. 225

to equivocation or to adopt strange face-saving devices in order to have his say without breaking the party discipline. When he had to concede his final defeat over the issue of office acceptance under the Government of India Act of 1935, he wrote his speech for the convention of all newly elected Congress members of provincial legislatures, before the All-India Congress Committee voted on the crucial resolution. After announcing that the speech had been written before he could know the decision by which he would, of course, abide, he used this opportunity to launch a final attack against the idea of office acceptance, and in this way he avoided commenting on a resolution which he knew only too well would seal the fate of his policy.[17] But in spite of all these humiliating reverses he served the Congress as a general secretary and thrice as its president in this important decade. He paid the price of leadership, but was it worth paying so much for being in office and not in power? This question must be answered in the wider context of the political trends of that time.

In the years after his return from Europe Nehru missed no opportunity of exploring all avenues of radicalism with a view to spreading the message of socialism and to strengthening the National Movement while giving it a leftist slant at the same time. He presided over many conferences of the newly founded Youth Leagues, he addressed the Kisan Sabhas (peasant organizations) and the Trade Union Congress. As a practical politician, he knew that it was neither possible nor perhaps desirable to merge all these organizations with the national movement, but he wanted to achieve some degree of joint action and advocated some kind of affiliation of these organizations with the Congress, preferably by means of functional representation.[18] For this he could only work if he held high office in the Congress. He was also aware of the complete disarray of the forces on the left. The Communists held aloof from the National Movement, because they were under orders from Moscow. Much of their strength had been sapped when the government arrested most of their prominent labour leaders. The labour movement was splitting up: Nehru had the doubtful privilege of presiding over the Trade Union Congress of 1929 which saw the withdrawal of the reformist right wing from the T.U.C., because this right wing was sick and tired of getting mixed up in the strikes organized by the revolutionary left.[19] Seen against this chaotic

[17] Presidential Address to the All-India Convention, Delhi, March 1937, in Nehru, *Eighteen Months in India*, p. 123
[18] See Nehru's article mentioned above in fn. 16
[19] For the proceedings of the All-India Trade Union Congress see *Indian Annual*

background Nehru's one-man campaign for socialism emerges as about the only consistent strand of socialist activity in those years.

As far as revolutionary potentialities were concerned, Nehru was quite sure that Gandhi and the Congress were the only force that could be relied upon. But he also knew that the Congress right wing was bound to lapse into halfheartedness after the end of a Gandhian campaign. The advance of fascism in Europe made him very apprehensive of similar developments in India, and from 1933 onward the connection between fascism and imperialism preoccupied his mind.[20] Through his persistent warnings most leftist nationalists were soon obsessed with the idea that the imperial power would strike a bargain with the Indian capitalists and thus detach the right wing from the National Movement. Nehru was therefore even more determined than ever before to work for the unity of the Congress and to sacrifice his own convictions to party discipline in order to prevent a split.

Nehru spent most of the early 1930s in prison. At the same time many leaders of the younger generation made use of their stay in prison for analysing their political position and discussing new points of departure. Marxism of a more determined brand than Nehru's emotional socialism was bred in these prison days. Young Bengal found the way from "terrorist individualism" to "disciplined communism".[21] At Nasik, Maharashtra, a group of socialists in their early thirties arrived at the conclusion that they should establish a truly socialist party as soon as they got out of jail. This party, the Congress Socialist Party, was founded in 1934 at Patna. The friend, philosopher and guide of the new party was Acharya Narendra Deva, a scholarly Marxist who was about Nehru's age, and thus about ten years senior to the group of founding fathers of the new party.[22]

Nehru was released from prison long after the new party was founded. Since his stay in prison had relieved him of the responsibility of participating in the establishment of the new party, he found it now less difficult to remain aloof from it while sympathizing with its programme. He included some of its members in the Working Committee of the Congress when he became the Congress president

---

Register (Calcutta, 1929), vol. ii, pp. 424 ff. See also R. R. Bakhale, "Trade Union Unity" in *The Servant of India*, 21 August 1930

[20] J. Nehru, *Whither India?* (Allahabad, 1933). See also Nehru, *Eighteen Months in India*, pp. 75 ff.

[21] Kalpana Dutt, *Chittagong Armoury Raiders*, Bombay, 1945

[22] Hari Kishore Singh, *A History of the Praja Socialist Party* (Lucknow, 1959), pp. 16 ff.

once more,[23] but he preferred to continue his individual crusade for socialism rather than identifying himself with the new party.

The Congress Socialist Party increased the leverage of the left wing in the Congress but it also heightened the apprehensions of the right wing and made it close its ranks. Nehru was apparently watching the trend of affairs in order to find out which of these two tendencies would assert itself more intensively.

The main issue was obviously the establishment of an alternative leadership in the Congress, but it was doubtful whether this aim could be achieved by the left wing in terms of an organized group like the Congress Socialist Party, or by means of a slow process of informal consolidation. M. N. Roy, who had been released from prison in 1936, advocated the latter method. Nehru's point of view was not entirely clear. He emphasized the analogy between the Congress Socialists and the extremists of pre-Gandhian days. Like the Moderates who seceded from the Congress and turned into the innocuous Liberal Party after 1919, the right wing of the Congress might shrink and isolate itself until it could be dispensed with.[24] But this vision of a decaying right wing did not tally with Nehru's apprehensions of the dangerous right wing which might enter into a fascist compact with the imperial power. These conflicting projections may explain Nehru's ambivalent attitude towards the C.S.P. This was matched by an equally ambivalent attitude of the C.S.P. towards Nehru, who was their mentor but not a member of their party. Actually they left much of their work to him and trusted that he, as the Congress president, would accomplish more in the crusade for socialism than any of the party members. Sampurnanand complained in 1936 that the C.S.P. was hibernating, leaving its work to Nehru, who was not a member of the party and therefore could not speak for it.[25]

So it was once more Nehru who carried the message of socialism to the Indian people while the avowed representatives of socialism tried hard to keep up with him and often failed to match his efforts, even though they may have surpassed him in ideological rigour.

III

The most important of Nehru's socialist achievements was un-

[23] Nehru, *Eighteen Months in India*, pp. 6–8

[24] J. Nehru, "Congress and Socialism", in Nehru, *Eighteen Months in India*, pp. 29 ff.

[25] Sampurnanand's address at the Kerala Socialist Conference, June 1936, in *Indian Annual Register* (Calcutta, 1936), vol. i, p. 348

doubtedly his success in getting the Congress to adopt a rudimentary economic programme at a fairly early stage. This programme was by no means revolutionary, but when independence was achieved, these early commitments had almost acquired the dignity of an ancient heritage. Nehru's main difficulty was to convince Gandhi of the necessity of such a programme, because Gandhi disliked generalities unless they could be linked with an immediate plan of action. However, as Gandhi had listed eleven points in 1929 which he considered to be "the substance of independence", Nehru could seize upon these points and elaborate a catalogue of fundamental and economic rights which was adopted by the session of the Indian National Congress at Karachi in 1931.

Gandhi's eleven points were carefully selected planks of an agitational platform on which "the classes and the masses" could unite. The important economic points of Gandhi's demands were: the devaluation of the rupee from 1s. 6d. to 1s. 4d.; the reduction of the land revenue by 50 per cent; the abolition of the salt tax; the reduction of the expenses for the army by 50 per cent; a cut in the salaries of the higher ranks of the civil service; and a protective tariff on imported textiles.[26] Most of these points corresponded to the demands of the Federation of Indian Chambers of Commerce, whose spokesman, G. D. Birla, endorsed Gandhi's views.[27] There was no socialism in this 'substance of independence'. The very cautiously phrased demands of the Karachi resolution were therefore a definite advance. In particular the right of a living wage, the introduction of an inheritance tax and of a graduated income tax on agricultural income, rent reduction, and state ownership or control of basic industries, were demands which reflected socialist influence. These demands were amalgamated with the list of fundamental rights contained in the Nehru Report of 1928 and with Gandhi's eleven points.[28] In this way the whole list came to be known as a catalogue of fundamental rights, although only some of the points correspond to fundamental rights in the constitutional sense of the term. The emphasis on fundamental rights was also supposed to assure the minorities and act as an antidote

[26] *Indian Annual Register* (Calcutta, 1930), vol. i, p. 24

[27] Text of Birla's speech at the conference of the Federation of the Indian Chambers of Commerce in *Indian Annual Register* (Calcutta, 1930), vol. i, p. 390

[28] Motilal Nehru *et al.*, *Report of the All Parties Conference Committee* (Allahabad, 1928), pp. 101–3. For the Karachi Resolution of the Indian National Congress see *Indian Annual Register* (Calcutta, 1931), vol. i, pp. 249 ff.; for an analysis of this resolution see D. R. Gadgil, "The Economic Programme of the Congress", in *The Servant of India*, 17 September 1931

to communal apprehensions. As a mildly socialist and decidedly anti-communal programme the Karachi resolution became the basis of the Congress election manifesto of 1936[29] and the main contribution of Indian nationalism to the Indian Constitution of 1950, which otherwise retained most of the paragraphs of the Government of India Act of 1935. For the purposes of the constitution the heterogeneous catalogue had to be divided into justiciable and non-justiciable rights, the latter being called directive principles of state policy.[30] Thus the Karachi resolution with all its shortcomings was a milestone on the way of India's political development.

Compared with the economic programme of the Congress Socialist Party the Karachi resolution appears, of course, rather insipid. The Congress Socialists demanded the transfer of power to the producing masses, socialization of all key industries with a view to the progressive socialization of all the instruments of production, distribution and exchange, the state monopoly of foreign trade, the elimination of princes and landlords and all other classes of exploiters, the encouragement of co-operative and collective farming by the state, and the liquidation of debts owed by peasants and workers. In order to create the political conditions for this programme they demanded adult franchise on a functional basis and a constituent assembly, to be convened after the capture of power and elected by local committees of deputies of workers, peasants and other exploited classes.[31] In many of these points they were sure of Nehru's support, as Nehru himself constantly emphasized the need of a constituent assembly based on adult franchise and as he was also in favour of functional representation. But he felt that it was more important to induce the vast Congress organization to adopt an economic point of view than to enhance the ideological integrity of a small left wing group.

The introduction of an economic element into the main stream of Congress nationalism was a rather frustrating endeavour, because the rank and file of the members and even many of the leaders had no idea of economic affairs and were satisfied with old slogans like "Drain of Wealth" and other simple theories which reduced economic exploitation to something that was exclusively practised by the foreign

---

[29] For the Congress Election Manifesto, see *Indian Annual Register* (Calcutta, 1934), vol. ii, pp. 220–1

[30] Cf. Constitution of India, §§ 36–51; see also B. N. Rau, *India's Constitution in the Making* (Bombay, 1960), pp. 232 ff.

[31] All-India Congress Socialist Party, *Constitution, Programme, and Resolutions of the Second Conference of the Party* (Bombay, 1935), pp. 7–8

colonial power. They were also not very attentive as to the content
of general resolutions and passed them without giving much thought
to them. From the time of his return to India in 1927, Nehru noticed
that he could get many radical resolutions passed which were not
understood by those who adopted them. Often he found that ideas
which had been embodied in earlier resolutions were vigorously
opposed at a later date. As early as 1929 the All-India Congress
Committee had stated:

"In the opinion of this Committee, the great poverty and misery
of the Indian people are due not only to the foreign exploitation of
India but also to the economic structure of the society, which the
alien rulers support so that their exploitation may continue. In
order therefore to remove this poverty and misery and to ameliorate
the condition of the Indian masses, it is essential to make revolutionary changes in the present economic and social structure of
society and to remove the gross inequalities."

But when Nehru spoke of revolutionary changes in 1936 in his address
as Congress president at the Lucknow session, many people thought
that he was introducing dangerous new ideas.[32] But in spite of these
experiences, Nehru felt that he could register some progress; the
Congress was not socialistic but it had ceased to be an organization
thinking in political terms only and ignoring economic issues, and now
conducted enquiries into peasant grievances and worked on an agrarian
programme. So the many years of half-understood propaganda and the
scores of absent-mindedly adopted resolutions did not seem to be
altogether wasted. The main question which Nehru had to answer
again and again was, of course, why there should be any discussion
about economic matters before the achievement of political independence, because such discussion would only split the ranks of the
nationalists and create confusion. Nehru's attitude toward this question
was ambivalent. In his answers he shifted his emphasis from time to
time. In 1933 when he wrote his famous article "Whither India?" he
pointed out that nationalism in Asia was appearing now in a socialist
garb, and that the national struggle for political freedom was slowly
turning into a social struggle for economic freedom. He concluded
that because of the world situation some nations in Asia might achieve
political and social emancipation simultaneously. In later years he
stressed once more the primacy of political independence and did not

[32] J. Nehru, *Eighteen Months in India*, p. 35

emphasize the idea of simultaneous emancipation in the political and economic spheres. Socialism was seen as a corrective of the political struggle, but not as its driving force: "The socialist state may be a dream of the distant future", but "socialism is a beacon light of the present, lighting up the path which we have to tread." [33]

[33] J. Nehru, *Eighteen Months in India*, p. 41

CONTRIBUTORS

S. N. MUKHERJEE: He was educated in Calcutta and London. He was Agatha Harrison Research Fellow at St Antony's College for 1963–64 and now he is a University Assistant Lecturer in the History of South Asia in the University of Cambridge. His book *"Sir William Jones and the Beginnings of Indology: an essay on the eighteenth-century British attitudes towards India"* is expected to be published shortly by the Cambridge University Press.

D. ARGOV: He was educated at the School of Oriental and African Studies, University of London. He is at present a lecturer in modern Indian History at the Institute of Asian and African Studies in the Hebrew University of Jerusalem. His book *"Moderates and Extremists in the Indian Nationalist Movement"* is to be published in August 1966 by Asia Publishing House.

DENNIS DALTON: He was educated in the State University of New Jersey, Chicago University and the School of Oriental and African Studies, University of London. In 1960–61 he visited Nepal as United States delegate of an agricultural programme. He is at present lecturer in Indian political thoughts at the School of Oriental and African Studies, London.

JOHANNES H. VOIGT: He studied History, English and Law at the Universities of Kiel and Marburg. He was a visiting lecturer in German language and Modern European History at Banares Hindu University, Kasividyafith and Punjab University, Chandigarh. At present he is a research scholar at St Antony's College writing a thesis on 'Nationalism in Indian Historical writings 1870–1920'.

S. GOPAL: He studied History at Balliol College, Oxford. He is at present the Director of Historical Research, Ministry of External Affairs, Government of India. He is author of *The Permanent Settlement in Bengal*, *The Viceroyalty of Lord Ripon*, *The Viceroyalty of Lord Irwin*, and *British policy in India 1854–1905*.

ZAFAR IMAM: He studied Political Science at Aligargh Muslim University and the London School of Economics and Political Science. He completed his Ph.D. in 1964.

DIETMAR ROTHERMUND: He studied Philosophy and History at Marburg and Munich and American History at the University of Pennsylvania, Philadelphia. In 1962 he was a visiting Fellow in the History Department, Institute of Advanced Studies, Australian National University, Canberra. He is at present teaching Indian History at the South Asian Institute, Heidelberg. He is the author of *The Layman's progress—Religious and Political Experience in Colonial Pennsylvania, 1740–1770*, and *Die Politische Willenshidang in Indien 1900–1960*.

Date Due